Biography

92
AGA
THARP, LOUISE HALL
Louis Agassiz

5343

DATE DUE			
FEB 19			
SEP 25			
FEB 18			
FEB 11 '82			
FEB 24 '82			
OCT 25			
DEC 13			
NO 14 '00			
			ALESCO

5343

✓

BOOKS BY
Louise Hall Tharp

CHAMPLAIN: NORTHWEST VOYAGER

COMPANY OF ADVENTURERS
The Story of the Hudson's Bay Company

THE PEABODY SISTERS OF SALEM

UNTIL VICTORY
Horace Mann and Mary Peabody

THREE SAINTS AND A SINNER
Julia Ward Howe
Louisa, Annie and Sam Ward

TORY HOLE

ADVENTUROUS ALLIANCE
The Story of the Agassiz Family of Boston

LOUIS AGASSIZ: ADVENTUROUS SCIENTIST

LOUIS
AGASSIZ
Adventurous Scientist

LOUIS AGASSIZ
Adventurous Scientist

BY
LOUISE
HALL
THARP

Illustrated by Rafaello Busoni

LITTLE, BROWN
AND COMPANY
Boston · Toronto

CONTENTS

LOUIS
AGASSIZ
Adventurous Scientist

Fishing on the Lake

IT WAS EARLY MORNING in midsummer and the Lake of Morat shone in the sun. Vineyards with walls around them stretched down to the water's edge with here and there a narrow road leading to a wharf. This was Switzerland and so there were mountain ranges rising across the lake, their peaks forever white with snow. A small house with many balconies stood near the lake shore, and on an upper balcony a boy sat at a table. In front of him were a book, quill pen and ink, and a notebook with his name written on the cover — *Jean Louis Rodolphe Agassiz.*

In Switzerland, people liked to give a child many names and then choose one to call him by. The Agassiz (pronounced Ag'a-see) family called this boy Louis. His father was pastor of the little church and also teacher in the village school of Môtier, where Louis was born. But Louis Agassiz was not in school, although school was in session. His father taught him at home. School vacation would be in the autumn at Môtier, when the children could help harvest the grapes. Louis would have a little time off then, too, but for the most part he studied harder than other boys his age. Louis Agassiz was born May 28, 1807 and he was now not much over nine years

old, but he could read and write in Latin. The big
book in front of him belonged to his father. It was in
Greek.

Louis wrote out his translation as fast as he dared, at
the same time taking pains to make his handwriting
small and neat. This was not a day to risk a blot, for
there would be no time for copying. He looked anxiously
over the balcony railing into the village street. Yes —
they were coming now. A small fishing boat was tied
up at the wharf below and two fishermen were beginning to climb the hill. Louis wrote the last line of his
assignment with extra care, then down the stairs he ran,

book and notebook in hand. He knocked at the door of
his father's study.

The Reverend Mr. Agassiz looked over his son's notebook carefully and smiled. "This is very good," he said.
"Now let me hear the passages you have learned by heart
for today. Pronounce carefully."

Louis liked this part of the lesson the best. He
had been reading about the famous march of the Greek
army under Xenophon, their general. "And the Greeks
cried out, 'The sea! The far-sounding sea!'" Louis
recited, enjoying every word. "Father, what does the
sea really look like? When am I going to see it, too?" he
asked.

Mr. Agassiz shook his head. "I myself have never seen
an ocean," he replied. "Someday you may travel as far
as the Lake of Geneva, which is all of forty miles long —
that should be water enough for you. Meanwhile, try to
be content with your lot."

At this point, there came a knock at the study door.
"It is Pierre and Jacques, the two fishermen," exclaimed
Louis. "Now please, Father, say yes."

"How do you know who it is? I'm to say yes to what?"
Mr. Agassiz wanted to know. But Louis was already ush-
ering in his two friends, members of his father's church
in Môtier.

Pierre, the elder of the two, nervously turned his cap
in his hands. But he came right to the point. "We would

like to take your son Louis out in our boat with us, sir —
with your permission."

"Well — it is true that he has done his lessons," said
Louis's father. "But the boy would be in your way, I
should think."

"Oh no, sir," said Jacques eagerly. "He has helped us
already while we were getting our boat ready for the
water after the ice melted. We have taught him to calk
the hull, mend nets and tar ropes. And now we have
promised to teach him all we know about fishing. By
your leave, sir, of course."

"Very well then," sighed Mr. Agassiz. "It does seem
to me that my Louis has strange tastes. But take him if
you will."

"Often we start at dawn," put in Pierre. "Would it
be permitted for him to come with us then?"

"Yes, yes, any time," said the boy's father. "Only lessons are not to be neglected," he reminded Louis.

Down the stairs dashed Louis Agassiz, stopping in his
mother's kitchen to beg the use of a wooden pail and to
put some bread and cheese in his pocket. His mother was
sitting at her spinning wheel on a lower balcony over-
looking the garden. "I will bring in lake trout for supper," Louis promised her.

"They will be welcome," smiled his mother. Although
there were village girls to help in the kitchen and men
to work in the vineyard that belonged to the minister,

the family had very little money to spend. Louis was the oldest child, with a brother Augustus two years younger and two sisters younger still. Mrs. Agassiz spent many hours at her spinning wheel because the fine yarn she made could be sold at Morat, the market town across the lake.

Louis ran down the steep cobblestoned street to the wharf and jumped aboard *L'Hirondelle* (the *Swallow*). Her name was French because he and his family and most of the people in Môtier spoke French. He helped to raise the sails which were fastened to a long pole called a gaff. There were two sails, each with a gaff nearly as long as the boat itself and much longer than the stumpy masts. A light breeze drew them out from shore and they began to cast their nets — Louis doing just as his fishermen friends told him. "He learns fast," they said of him proudly.

When the nets were pulled in and the shining, slippery mass of fish was stowed in the bottom of the boat, the fishermen gave Louis some of the best of their catch to take home. But they laughed when he asked to keep a few that they were about to throw back into the lake. "It's just that they are so pretty," Louis explained. "Look at this one. On its back and sides are big pink spots with light blue rings around them. I never saw one like this before."

"Well, a fish is a fish," said Pierre.

And Jacques agreed. "Either you can eat them or you can't." But they let Louis keep as many of these small fish as he wanted.

"They are pretty, at that," said Jacques, looking more closely. "Here. I'll dip your bucket overside for you and fill it with water so you can keep your fish alive."

At noon, Louis and his friends ate their lunch on the deck of the small fishing boat. "Nine months winter and three months cold," people said of the mountain villages of Switzerland, but in the central plateau where Louis Agassiz lived the sun shone hot in summer. The land was

fertile and the grapes that grew around Môtier were made into a famous wine. But in the hot sunshine the fish swam deep and there seemed to be little use in casting the net. Louis had time to admire the fish in his pail.

"Look, there are at least three different kinds here," he exclaimed. "What are their names?"

"Oh, they're just minnows," said Pierre.

"Well, they do have different names," said Jacques thoughtfully. "That gray one there with the red below is called *l'ombre chevalier* — the shadowy horseman."

"Oh, no, just 'the shadow,' " corrected Pierre. "And over on the lake at Neuchâtel, not five miles from here, they call it 'red trout.' "

"Maybe there's a book telling all the right names," suggested Louis. But his fishermen friends thought not.

The breeze had dropped and now the fishermen got out the long oars to row home. The Lake of Morat was only four miles wide so that the shore looked near and Louis was pleased to be allowed to help pull an oar. "They say that on the ocean you can sail out of sight of land," he remarked. "I would love to do that, wouldn't you?"

The fishermen laughed. "How would you like to have to row home?" they asked.

"But think how many fish there must be in the ocean!" Louis insisted.

His friends were still unimpressed. "We have enough
to eat and a few to sell. We are quite content and so will
you be when you are a man," they said.

Seated with his back to the bow of the boat, Louis
could look eastward across the lake to the town of Morat
for which the lake was named. Beyond, he could see the
great ridges of the Bernese Oberland like a blue wall
against the sky. The Jungfrau (the "Young Girl") was
the most famous peak in that range and it was always
snow-capped. "Tell me, has anyone ever climbed the
Jungfrau?" Louis asked.

Again the fishermen laughed and it was Pierre who replied. "No, of course not. No one ever climbed it and
no one ever will."

"I might, someday," said Louis.

Jacques looked at the boy's eager face, dark eyes alight,
thick chestnut hair pushed back from a broad forehead.
There was something about Louis Agassiz that was different from other people. Louis was always thinking
about things and asking questions. At the same time, he
was always doing something. People like that are apt
to have adventures.

"Listen to the boy!" exclaimed Pierre. "First he wants
to see a great ocean and catch all the fish. Next he wants
to climb the Jungfrau!"

"Perhaps someday he'll do all that and more," said
Jacques. "He wants to find a book with the names of all

the fish in it, don't forget. Maybe he'll write down all their names himself. But will you come out with us again tomorrow, Louis? Tomorrow we start at dawn."

"I'll be waiting at the wharf," Louis promised.

$\mathcal{A}$ Boy's First Collection

LOUIS AGASSIZ went joyfully up the street trying not to slop too much water out of his wooden pail. He had ten handsome lake trout for his family dinner table and eight small fish of his own that nobody else wanted. Going through the gate in the garden wall, he presented his trout at the kitchen door. They were much admired. Then, pail still in hand, he went to the pool in the garden.

Almost everyone in Môtier had a garden pool, large or small. Each was made from a huge boulder having a natural hollow in it which, with mallet and stone-chisel, had been enlarged and deepened. The stone basin in the Agassiz garden was one of the best in town. It was filled with fresh spring water from a wooden pipe let into the hillside behind the house and the overflow from the pool made a trickle of a brook in the garden. Louis put his fish in this pool.

Augustus came running out into the garden, eager to hear all about his big brother's adventures on the lake. Louis was more than willing to make a good story of it, forgetting nothing. Together they admired the fish in the pool, but two had died and were floating upside down. "Maybe there wasn't enough water in my pail," said

Louis regretfully. They discussed the matter of feeding their new pets.

"Fish eat insects that swim on top of the water," Augustus remembered. "And I've seen them leap out of the water for flies. Then of course I can get them worms out of the garden." Later and a little to the surprise of both boys, they found that their fish would also eat finely cut up meat scraps and Augustus was the one who would try to acquire scraps — from a kitchen where nothing was ever wasted.

Louis scooped up his two dead fish and carried them up to his room. He was careful to avoid notice. His mother was a very neat housekeeper and she did not entirely approve of the things already in his room. She would be certain to object to dead fish.

As far as Louis Agassiz was concerned, his room suited him to perfection. There was his collection of birds' nests, nearly all of them found in the weeds along the lake shore. There were snake skins and the carefully dried remains of several frogs. And there was the cage with the squirrel in it — a pet with sharp teeth and a habit of using them. An empty cage had been the home of field mice but Louis kept them only in the winter and let them go in spring. On a shelf was a collection of minerals, most of them smooth pebbles. Two or three were black and these Louis especially prized. One was round and the others looked like large black beans. Someday, Louis

Agassiz would find out that these strange things were really fossils.

Right now, Louis's problem was what to do with two dead fish. Already their bright color had begun to fade. Louis could draw unusually well and he had a box of water colors which he shared with his sisters. A good portrait of these fish would be just the thing for his collection, so he sat down to see what he could do. But a careful and accurate portrait of a fish took time, as Louis soon discovered. And there was his Latin lesson for the next day, and his Greek, not to mention his arithmetic, which he hated. So he summoned his sister Cecile. She could draw and paint almost as well as he could and she was pleased to be allowed to help her brother. Louis insisted that she put in just the right number of scales and get the spots exactly the right color. But he had a way of praising her when she did well so that she worked hard.

All summer long, whenever his lessons were done, Louis Agassiz went out with the fishermen. His arms and shoulders grew strong so that he could pull an oar alone or raise a sail without help. He could haul in a net as well as Pierre or Jacques and they proudly said that they had taught him all they knew. He brought home fine lake trout for his mother and many strange small fish for himself. Both he and his sister industriously painted

pictures and soon he hoped to have a portrait of every
kind of fish in the Lake of Morat.

Louis was not satisfied, however. He found the skeleton of a fish on the shore of the lake one day and it was
interesting. It had a skull, a backbone and ribs — all in
their proper places and not in a pile like fish bones on a
plate. Louis thought that if he could clean bones nicely
and glue them to a board they would make a fine addition
to his collection. This proved much harder to do than
he had supposed, but he kept trying until finally he could
mount a fish skeleton quite well. And now he discovered
a strange thing. Some of the fish that had different colors
had bones just alike, except that some were small and
others larger. These fish changed their colors as they
grew older! Here was something new to tell Jacques and
Pierre.

There were many days when Louis could not go out
fishing because he got so interested in his fish skeletons
that he did not finish his Greek. And finally there came
the sad day when his father said he could not go out any
more at all. "You were not born to be a fisherman," said
Mr. Agassiz, who was sometimes very severe. "You are
to go into the office of a merchant and keep his accounts.
Of course you will never be rich, but you will lead a
far easier life than that of your friends the fishermen."

Louis knew better than to argue with his father, and

it was his mother who came to his rescue. "As to fish," she said mildly, "have you seen the fish bones Louis mounts on wood? It calls to mind my father, who used to study such things."

"We have no money to send Louis to school to learn to be a doctor like your father," said Mr. Agassiz.

Mrs. Agassiz considered bringing up the point that her brother was also a doctor and might help Louis. But she decided to wait a while.

As for Louis, he was much cast down because he had enjoyed every moment with his friends the two fishermen. He did not see how he was ever going to get at least one of every kind of fish in the Lake of Morat. But he soon made a discovery. By wading into the water on the lake shore and then standing very still, he and his brother could catch fish with their hands, without a net or a line. It was just a matter of patience and then of quickness. The fishermen, Pierre and Jacques, stopped by one day to watch the boys. They were astonished and they told all the neighbors about the Agassiz boys.

Summer was a wonderful time on the Lake of Morat but early autumn was better still. The grapes ripened and from other parts of Switzerland where no grapes grew came men to help with the harvest. These people were called "vintners." They always came to the same towns year after year and camped out in the vineyards where they worked. They were greeted as old friends.

Some of them had married girls from Môtier, who would come with them and bring the children, visiting parents and introducing young cousins to each other. Now it was school vacation time and although the children helped with the harvest, it was a playtime too. Even the Agassiz boys were allowed to put aside their books.

When work was over in the evening there was music and square-dancing with almost everyone in town joining in. Children were allowed to drink the fresh grape juice as it came from the presses and nothing ever tasted half so good. There were great baskets full of grapes in all the houses and children were welcome to help themselves to all they wanted.

Each year at this time a man called a cooper went from house to house making barrels in which to store the wine. He brought staves with him which he had cut and shaped from small oak trees during the winter months. The staves were to be bound together with hoops, and a "head" would be fitted to each end. At the Agassiz house as at all the others, the cooper set up barrels for the wine which was to be stored in the cellar and for the wine which would be sold for much-needed cash. Louis watched the cooper carefully. Then he carved out small staves, hooped and headed them for himself.

Also traveling from house to house was the shoemaker. He would patch shoes if he could. But Louis always outgrew his shoes. He would be a tall man someday and every year Augustus had to wear his older brother's shoes while Louis had new ones made. He put his foot on the sole leather and watched the shoemaker draw around it. Then came a pattern for the uppers, to be made from sturdy but much lighter leather, then the cutting and the stitching, with Louis looking on. He asked for a few scraps of leather and made a pair of shoes for his sister's doll. They were very nicely done, the shoemaker said.

The Reverend Mr. Agassiz was not especially pleased when Louis learned to make things. A clerk in a merchant's office would have no need to be skillful with his hands, he argued. Louis should pay more attention to his arithmetic. And if Louis's mother brought up the point that a surgeon like her brother needed skillful fingers — the question of money still remained. Louis might be even more skillful than his uncle but schooling was too expensive.

Not all the autumn visitors were artisans. There was the man with the cheese cart, for example. He had a horse and a long narrow cart just wide enough to hold a wheel-shaped piece of cheese and long enough to carry twenty or thirty such cheeses. The man with the cheese cart knew wonderful things and he was willing to talk to a boy who asked good questions. The cheese vendor had been in the "alps." But by this he did not mean the whole mountain ranges — he meant only the high pastureland where the grass grew rich and green as soon as the snow melted. Here herds of cattle, sheep and goats were led in springtime and here the herders and their families lived all summer. Each village in the valley had an "alp" or pastureland assigned to it and to each family in the village a certain space belonged, year after year.

High above the "alps" the mountain peaks were covered with snow, summer and winter. "Have you ever climbed the Jungfrau?" Louis asked the man who came by with cheese for sale.

"No indeed, I never have time for that," the man replied. "The herdsmen bring me milk and I am always busy at the little house where I make my cheese." The cheesemaker had nevertheless ventured once upon a great glacier, a river of ice and snow in a valley below the summits of the Alps. There were crevasses, he said — deep cracks in the ice where a man might fall hundreds of feet and never be seen again. These things he knew, and Louis listened to his stories with mounting excitement.

Switzerland is only two hundred and twenty-six miles long and one hundred and thirty-seven miles wide at its widest point. But it seemed large to Louis Agassiz and for a good reason. High mountains kept the people who lived in the valleys from traveling very far and from visiting each other very often. There were no trains when Louis was a boy. Each of the many lakes in the valley had its village, some large, some small, in which the customs of the people were different. People even dressed differently, so that if you knew about such things, you could tell where a woman came from by the shape of her hat and you could name a boy's village by the cut and color of his coat. Louis Agassiz was never tired of questioning travelers about the world beyond his own small village of Môtier.

"What kinds of rocks are there in the Alps?" he asked the cheese vendor. "Could you remember to bring me a few for my collection when you come by next year?"

The cheese seller laughed. "Most of the rocks are much

too big," he said, "but I'll see what I can do. I've seen
many like the one your garden pool is made from and I
have seen smooth, round rocks that were larger still.
They were scattered around in a pasture as if a giant had
been playing marbles."

"Now I would like to see that!" exclaimed Louis.
"How do you suppose they got there? And why are they
here too — so far away?"

But the cheese seller shrugged his shoulders. "A flood,
maybe. That's what people say." It was a question he
really couldn't answer, but it was a question that Louis
Agassiz would someday answer for himself.

3

Louis Makes Plans

LOUIS AGASSIZ could never remember a time when he did not long to see the world beyond his own village. He made one brave attempt before he was old enough to go away to school. It was early in the winter and a sudden cold wave had come before the first heavy snowfall. The Lake of Morat was frozen as smooth as glass.

Louis had been kept in the house to do his arithmetic and somehow the answers would not come out right. His father had driven off with the horse and two-wheeled cart, taking the yarn his wife had spun, to sell on market day at Morat. Louis longed to go but knew better than to ask — with lessons still unfinished.

To make matters worse, there were the shouts of other boys and girls out on the ice. Louis erased, corrected and erased. He showed his mother his sums until at last she said that they were right. By then, it was nearly noon.

Out of the house dashed Louis, his skates banging against his legs as he tore down the cobblestoned street to the lake. Right behind him came his brother Augustus, always a little slower in his studies than Louis, but better at arithmetic and now also free to play. The boys strapped on their skates, and almost before he knew it, Louis was far from shore. "Wait for me!" called Augustus and Louis felt impatient. But he always hated to see anyone unhappy, so he cut a few figure eights and waited until his little tag-along brother caught up.

Then on went the boys, the wind at their backs making them feel as though they were flying. When they looked behind, they saw that most of their friends had gone home. Ahead of them, the town of Morat looked wonderfully close. There was a wall around it, a castle on a hill, and a great gate. "We could go on and find Father and he would take us home in the cart," suggested Louis tentatively.

"We would see the fair," said Augustus, his eyes shining. "We could see some of the toys they make over there — all carved out of wood and painted in bright colors." Without exactly deciding the question of whether to go on or go home, the boys had been skating toward Morat. But now they saw a narrow strip of water ahead instead of ice.

Louis and Augustus had been skating almost due east to cross the lake at its narrowest point, but there was nothing for it now but to go either north or south in the hope of finding solid ice nearer shore. The strip of open water seemed to go on and on. At last it grew narrow. "Could you jump over it now?" Louis asked his brother. But Augustus was afraid.

Louis remembered something his friend the cheese vendor had told him. If two men were climbing a glacier and came to a crevasse, there was one thing they could do to get across. The crevasse had to be narrow and one man had to be very strong. Louis was always proud of his strength. "I'll make myself into a bridge for you," he proposed. "You can crawl over my back and then help me pull myself to the other side." Augustus was doubtful but agreed to try.

It was just at this point that Mrs. Agassiz put her eye to the telescope which her husband kept at his study window. She had not been anxious about her boys at first. After all, they had gone out to skate much later than their friends. But when one of the neighbor's children told her that Louis and Augustus were crossing the lake, she rushed up the stairs in alarm. She saw the open water first — then the boys.

A man was repairing the roof of the parsonage and Mrs. Agassiz called to him frantically. He had his skates with him, for he had come down the lake to work, using the ice for a highway as many people did. When she finally made him understand, he agreed to go out on the lake and bring the boys home.

Louis and Augustus Agassiz got safely over the crack in the ice and reached the eastern shore of Lake Morat. They were tired, so they sat down to rest on the end of a fisherman's wharf before going up to the town. Steep streets led to houses that seemed bigger than those at their home town of Môtier. There were more wooden balconies, all elaborately carved, some of them jutting out over the streets and having shops beneath. Louis and Augustus could see people going in and out of the town gate, dressed in their best for market day. There were boys in bright red coats and girls who wore embroidered kerchiefs over their heads. Somewhere, someone was playing music on a shepherd's pipe. This was going to be a great adventure and the Agassiz boys, although a little scared, were also much excited.

And then they noticed that a man was skating toward them. "It's old Jerome from our village," said Louis. "I thought he was going to mend our roof today."

"Have you come to the fair?" Augustus asked, as the workman slid to a stop in front of the wharf.

"I've come to take you home," said Jerome. And nothing the boys could say would make him change his tune. Two very tired boys skated back across the lake without seeing the fair.

The next time Louis Agassiz skated across the Lake of Morat he remembered to ask permission first. He often visited other towns and hamlets. But to a boy who had always longed to see the world, a few villages a few miles apart were not enough. It was wonderful news when his father told Louis that the time had come for him to go away to school.

Mr. Agassiz had chosen the College of Bienne for Louis. Although it was called a college, it was really a

high school and Louis was only ten years old. He would
be one of the younger boys in his class.

Louis felt very grown-up as he climbed into his father's two-wheeled cart. At his feet was a small box with
his clothes and a few books. His mother, Augustus and
his sisters stood at the garden gate and waved as Father's
white horse went clip-clopping down the street, and
Louis, who had been feeling gay, had suddenly a queer
lump in his throat.

The distance from Môtier to Bienne was only twenty
miles but it was a slow journey northward along the
bank of the Lake of Morat, then over a river and along
part of the Lake of Neuchâtel to the Lake of Bienne.
The Lake of Neuchâtel, when he caught a glimpse of it,
looked enormous to Louis. It was in fact nearly five times
the length of his own little Lake of Morat and twice as
wide.

Even the Lake of Bienne, tiny on any map, was nine
miles long and looked big to Louis Agassiz. But it was
the town itself which gave him one surprise after another. In the first place, everyone was speaking German.
Here was Louis only twenty miles from home and con-
fronted by a different language. It was confusing but
exciting and Louis found himself listening hard, watching people's faces and trying to guess what they said.
The town itself, which he had always called Bienne, was
called Biel in German, he discovered.

At the center of town the public square was called "The Ring." Knights once rode there. All the buildings around it were so old that they looked as though knights in armor ought to come strolling through the doors instead of Swiss watchmakers in sturdy homespun. There were clocks and watches in all the shop windows. In fact the whole town almost seemed to tick of its own accord, and Louis saw boys younger than himself sitting at benches fitting together tiny wheels. In all the houses dotting the countryside, whole families made parts of watches, Louis's father told him. These tiny screws and wheels and springs were brought to town and sold to master clockmakers who set their apprentices to work putting parts together.

There were vineyards near the lake like those in Môtier, but behind the town the land rose into foothills and beyond were mountains. There were tall pines such as Louis had never seen before. He felt sorry for the boys who must sit at benches all day and he resolved to visit the pine forest at once.

But the College of Bienne had one more surprise for Louis. He had supposed that his father made him study very hard and now he realized that he had been accustomed to a good deal of playtime. At his new school the boys worked nine hours a day. Lessons were interrupted by periods of outdoor exercise and Louis became very good at gymnastic drill. But there was no roaming in pine forests for boys at work in school.

At first, Louis was very lonely. All his classes were taught in German. All the other boys spoke German and he longed for a word of French. He missed his family, Augustus in particular, and he wrote to his brother to study hard so as to come to school with him the next year. This Augustus did and although he was two years

younger, Louis always helped him so that he could be in
all his brother's classes. Teaching people was fun, Louis
Agassiz discovered.

Most of the studies were in Latin and Greek with
French, German and Italian thrown in. Most of the work
was in memorizing and in writing translations and com-
positions in notebooks with never a blot or a word
scratched out. Louis was grateful now because his father
had trained him so carefully. He was ahead of most boys
in Latin and Greek. His father had made him speak perfect French so that Italian, being like French and Latin,
seemed easy. Louis hated to see other students get ahead
of him and he worked extra hard on German. Soon he
was speaking it so well that later, German friends would
be surprised to hear that Louis Agassiz had not spoken
German all his life.

Louis liked all his studies except bookkeeping — which
his father had sent him to school especially to learn. He
tried hard but somehow mistakes crept into his practice
ledgers and he never knew how they got there. What
Louis liked best of all right now, however, was vacation
time. He discovered that he had a wonderful family of
aunts, uncles and cousins whom he hardly knew at all.
They lived along the Lake of Neuchâtel and Louis got
acquainted with them all when he stayed with his Grandfather Mayor and his Aunt Lisette who lived in a big
house that was a family gathering place.

Easter was a time of great festivity around Neuchâtel. Louis helped his cousins color dozens of Easter eggs. On Easter Sunday everybody went to church and all the girls in the family wore masses of artificial flowers on their hats. Louis had never seen so gay a sight and he was sorry to hear that the flowers were worn only at Easter, then taken off the hats and put away until next year.

On Easter Sunday afternoon, the Neuchâtel villagers all gathered in the village square and the races started. Two boys in white costumes trimmed with bright-colored ribbons marched to the square, led along by musicians. Easter eggs had been laid out at intervals on the ground as in a potato race — but a long one. At a signal, one boy began to run to the next village. He would try to get there before the other boy picked up all the eggs. Louis loved the gay costumes and would have liked to wear one. He was a fast runner himself and wished he might have been in the race, but it was good news to hear that after the race everyone would gather in front of his grandfather's house.

Louis hurried back to the big house and stood on the balcony with Dr. Mayor and the rest of the family. All the villagers gathered below and a man made a speech which Louis could not understand. He was much surprised and a little cross with himself, but his Aunt Lisette explained that the speech was in the local "patois." And seeing that the boy was interested, Louis's grand-

father told him that the language was very old and that
something like it had been spoken in Switzerland before
the days of the Romans.

Next came a square dance especially in honor of the
doctor and his family. Louis was delighted to find that
all his cousins were going to be in it and that he could
dance in it too. One of his cousins showed him the steps
while they all dressed in gay costumes brought down
from the attic. Louis thought it would be fun to dress
like that all the time, but his cousins said that only
country people wore peasant costumes. Louis had never
had so much fun in his life.

Best of all were the rides he took with his grandfather
behind the old white horse. Dr. Mayor was the only
physician for miles around and there was plenty of time
for talk as he made his rounds visiting his patients.
Louis discovered that his grandfather was interested in
collections — of stones, of birds' nests, but particularly
of bones. And Dr. Mayor was amused and pleased when
Louis showed his skill at catching a fish with his bare
hands. "Now tonight," said the doctor, "I'll show you
a thing or two about mounting bones. To be sure, fish
bones are a little out of my line but you have just the
hands for it."

It was a most wonderful present when his grandfather
gave Louis a small, sharp knife. "Here is your first scal-
pel," Dr. Mayor said. He was pleased to see how quickly

Louis learned his first lesson in dissection. It was not enough, Louis Agassiz decided, to count a fish's scales, notice their color, nor even to mount its bones. You must also find out about its lungs, its liver and how it laid eggs.

The long vacation came in the autumn. Then Louis, and after the first year Augustus too, walked home to Môtier. They had no money to waste on stagecoach fare and, besides, the road led through marshland. There were frogs and birds' nests, turtles and a few snakes to be discovered and caught if possible. But the boys always remembered that the road home seemed short and the road back to school a long one.

When Louis Agassiz was fourteen he had "learned all his notebooks" at the College of Bienne. This meant that he could recite page after page by heart. All his life people would marvel at his wonderful memory. His father's plan for him had not changed and Louis knew that he must do as he was told. But he could not help making plans for himself.

"I will serve my apprenticeship in commerce at Neuchâtel for a year and a half," he wrote his father.

Then he told of his own plan. "I wish to advance in the sciences," he said. "I should like to pass four years at a university in Germany and finally finish my studies in Paris where I would stay about five years. Then, at the age of twenty-five, I could begin to write."

Louis did not say what kind of books he planned to write but at the age of fourteen he already knew more than most people about fresh-water fish. His first books would tell about them.

Louis Agassiz's father was proud of him. But a university education and graduate studies in Paris would cost a great deal of money. The Reverend Mr. Agassiz had to tell his son to put away boyish dreams and to try to be practical.

4

The Young Scientist

LOUIS AGASSIZ'S UNCLE, François Mayor, agreed to take him into his office at Neuchâtel and Louis's fate seemed sealed. But the teachers at the College of Bienne wrote to Louis's father and to his grandfather. Louis had some of the highest marks in school. It was a pity that such a good student should become a clerk so soon. Why not send the boy to a university at least for a year or two?

It was the good Dr. Mayor, Louis's grandfather, who thought of a way to help both Louis and Augustus. On the Lake of Neuchâtel there was a village called Orbe. It was larger than Môtier where Louis was born. The people at Orbe needed a pastor for their church and a teacher for their school and they could pay a good salary. Dr. Mayor had patients in Orbe. He spoke a word in favor of the Reverend Mr. Agassiz and in 1821, the year that Louis was fourteen, the whole family moved to Orbe. They had a larger house, a better vineyard, fruit trees and a fine vegetable garden. Now both Louis and Augustus could stay in school. The family chose the University of Lausanne for them and for a good reason. Mrs. Agassiz's brother, Dr. Mathias Mayor, was a well-to-do surgeon at Lausanne and he could provide a home for the boys.

Lausanne, on the Lake of Geneva, is only about thirty-five miles from Orbe — in a straight line on a map. But there were no airplanes and it was a complicated trip, first by boat along the Lake of Neuchâtel and then by winding valley roads in a horse-drawn public coach called a diligence. Augustus, who was twelve, would have been lonely and a little homesick on what seemed a long journey — except that Louis was so cheerful. Louis laughed at his brother's solemn face and sang snatches of song all off key until Augustus found himself laughing too. They persuaded a friendly cheese vendor to give them a lift in his cart part of the way, to save diligence fare.

Now at last Louis Agassiz saw the Lake of Geneva. It was a deeper blue than any other lake he had ever seen and it curved away out of sight so that it seemed very large as his father had promised. But the opposite shore was near, for the lake was narrow, and Louis still longed for a glimpse of open ocean.

Courses at the university proved easy for Louis because he had the habit of hard study. The language was French and both boys were glad because it made them feel more at home. But there were many foreign students and for the first time Louis met boys from other countries. Many were English and Louis promptly began to pick up a little English. He loved to talk to everyone he met and in their own language if possible.

Lausanne was the first real city Louis Agassiz had ever seen and it was an exciting one. Steep streets mounted from terrace to terrace and fine views of Mont Blanc attracted tourists. The air was so fresh and clear that people came to Lausanne for their health and there were theaters for the amusement of all these visitors. The Agassiz boys had to be careful of their money but they did not miss all the chances to have a good time. Uncle Mathias was generous with his own family and with his nephews as well.

But Louis, exploring the city one day, made a discovery more important to him than the magic of a theater. Tucked away in an old building on a square just below the cathedral, he found a natural history museum. It was the first real museum he had ever seen. It had only one room with an office behind it. There were shelves all around the walls on which were stones. In a cabinet in the middle of the room were stones, tan in color, and the shapes of tiny shells seemed to be molded into them. And there were gray-colored rocks set with shining black objects, some of which were round like eyes and some shaped like beans. Louis felt a thrill of excitement. He had three such black "pebbles" himself in his own collection. But these in the museum were set in gray stone in a sort of pattern which reminded him of the way a fish's teeth might be arranged.

Louis had no idea how long he had been in the museum when a pleasant-looking gentleman came out of the office. He walked to the display cabinet where Louis was standing, and afterwards it occurred to Louis that he had come to say it was closing time for the museum. But Louis spoke first. "I beg your pardon, sir," he said, "but could you tell me what these black bean-shaped stones are?"

The stranger smiled. "The country people call them 'petrified beans,' " he said. "The round ones are commonly called 'eyes' and people keep them for good-luck stones. They are found in sandstone quarries not far from Neuchâtel. Now tell me, young man, what do you suppose they really are?"

"Well," said Louis, a little afraid of being laughed at, "they somehow remind me of the teeth of fish — except it would have to be a huge fish."

"Why not?" countered the stranger. "They tell me that the Czar of Russia has the bones of a huge animal found stuck in the ice in Siberia. So why not huge fish in Switzerland — before history began of course. But how came you to make so close a guess, my boy? Some of my friends will dispute you — but I think you are right."

Louis found himself telling the stranger all about his collection of fish back home. They moved from shelf to shelf and from case to case in the small, crowded room.

Louis asked questions and his new friend could answer some but not all of them. *Salmo* was the Latin name for salmon, Louis learned. The lake trout he knew so well belong to the salmon family. The "shadowy horseman" or "red trout" which he had studied by himself was described by Linnaeus, a famous botanist, but many other fish had never been described.

"Insects are my specialty," Louis's friend explained. "Few people know much about fish. No one has so far found any more of the giant fish than these fossil teeth, so we have no idea how big he really was. Science needs an ichthyologist. Perhaps you are the man."

The fourteen-year-old Louis Agassiz had no trouble with the word "ichthyologist." He knew that it came from the Greek word meaning "fish" and he was much pleased with the idea that he might someday earn such a name.

At this point clocks began to strike from the many bell towers in Lausanne. They had struck several times before while the two were talking but neither of them heard. Now the gentleman exclaimed, "Can it be so late! I am dining with Monsieur the Doctor Mayor tonight."

"Then we can walk down the hill together," Louis said. "I am the doctor's nephew and I too shall be late. But it was my fault and I will take all the blame."

"Ah, my old friend Professor Chavannes is here at

last," exclaimed Dr. Mayor when the two friends finally appeared. He listened to Louis's explanation. "You shall be forgiven," he said, "since you have brought the professor."

"Never trust an entomologist," laughed Louis's aunt. "I supposed that you were studying one of your horrid insects and that you might not come at all. I'm glad it was Louis who kept you and not some sort of spider. Come in to dinner and let us hope for the best from a warmed-over meal."

That evening, when Augustus and their cousins set out for the theater, Louis stayed at home with his uncle and Professor Chavannes, director of the Natural History Museum of Lausanne. He was pleased to be included in the scientific conversation that went on at his uncle's house this evening and also during many evenings to come.

The Helvetic Society of Natural History had been started in nearby Geneva in 1816, about five years before Louis Agassiz came to Lausanne. He met many members at his uncle's house. There was Monsieur Jean de Charpentier, for example, director of the salt mines at Bex, about thirty miles from Lausanne. He told Louis about layers of different-colored earth lying one above the other far underground. Strata, he called them. He said there were two huge boulders at the entrance to the salt mine and Louis realized that they must be similar to the one in his father's garden in Môtier. "How did they get there?" Louis asked. But Monsieur de Charpentier did not know.

Professor Chavannes gave Louis the key to the museum and to the library in his office. "I wish I could answer all your questions," he said, "but my own studies keep me busy. Here are the books and there on the shelves are the specimens. You can learn for yourself."

At first, Augustus had not been as excited as Louis over the Natural History Museum. But Louis Agassiz had enthusiasm of a special kind. It was contagious and people around him found themselves sharing it. Soon the two boys spent all their spare time studying the collections and reading the books. They learned about the great Swedish botanist Linnaeus, who had lived about a hundred years before they were born. Linnaeus invented a system so that living things which resembled each other could be placed in "families." He gave each family a Latin name and then added other names telling more about each separate specimen. These names could include a word telling if the object was large or small, what color it was and where it was to be found. Names got rather long of course, but both Louis and Augustus had studied so much Latin that this never bothered them.

Linnaeus put his own name at the end of all the names of living things he had been the first to describe. "Perhaps my name will be in scientific books and on labels in museums someday," Louis said. He practiced writing his name in Latin. It would be "Agassii," he decided. It looked queer but it also made him feel proud.

"I shall need to own these books," Louis announced. "How else can I tell when I discover something new?"

"We could never afford to buy them," said Augustus, who was the more practical of the two.

"Then we must copy out the parts I am going to need the most," Louis decided, and of course Augustus agreed to help.

Even paper was a problem because it was expensive. The boys used every scrap they could find, writing on backs of letters, on blank pages in old account books given them by their aunt or bought for a few pennies from a junk dealer. They kept their writing as small as they could but took pains to write neatly so that every word could be read. Then they sewed their pages together to make books of their own.

Louis Agassiz now knew what he wanted to do with his life. "I am going to be the director of a natural history museum," he said. And since he always liked to do things in a big way, he decided to be the director of what was then the largest and finest museum in the world — the Jardin des Plantes in Paris.

The Jardin des Plantes (Botanical Garden) was started as a place to grow herbs that could be used as medicine. Then doctors began to realize that they could learn a great deal about human beings if they studied animals, and a zoo was added. Next came lecture halls and rooms where all sorts of collections were kept, and finally the Jardin des Plantes grew into a big natural history museum where people could study as at a college.

When Louis told his family about his plans his father was not happy. There were so very few natural history museums in the world that he did not see how a young man could hope to earn a living — the work would be so hard to find. As for being the head of the world's greatest museum — that was just a boy's dream. Louis must come back to Neuchâtel and be a clerk, his father said.

But in Switzerland a boy's whole family tried to help him decide on a career. Dr. Mathias Mayor had been teaching Louis the use of a microscope and had been giving him advanced lessons in dissecting. The boy had talent, his uncle said. Why not let Louis study medicine?

Louis remembered that the Jardin des Plantes had been started by doctors. He had read that the great Linnaeus had been a doctor at first and had begun his study of botany by trying to find herbs to use as medicine. Linnaeus had a country practice like Grandfather Mayor and he collected flowers while on his rounds to see his patients. So Louis did not give up his dream. It was true that he must earn a living and he felt very lucky indeed when his father said he could study medicine at the University of Zurich for two years. Augustus could go too and the Agassiz family would be proud if each boy became a doctor.

5

The Outside World

ZURICH was the largest city in Switzerland. The outlet of the Lake of Zurich, a fast-flowing torrent, ran through the center of town, and there were many bridges. As in Lausanne, the city rose sharply from the level of the lake in a series of natural terraces with fine views of snow-covered peaks. People enjoyed life in Zurich as they strolled along the wide streets with houses on one side only and a lake view on the other. In summer there were band concerts in the open air. German was the language and the Agassiz boys found they had not forgotten it.

The medical school at Zurich attracted many German students. They had come to learn all they could in the shortest possible time because most of them had little money. Louis and Augustus Agassiz worked just as hard and for the same good reason. But afterwards, when Louis wanted to describe someone who really knew how to study, he would say, "He works like a German student."

The young Germans played as hard as they worked and their favorite sport was mountain climbing. For the first time Louis found himself among people who felt the challenge of a mountain peak the way he did himself. When vacation time came, Augustus decided to go home but Louis joined some friends who were going up the Rigi. This mountain, five thousand nine hundred and five feet high, is now famous for its ski slopes. In Agassiz's time, it was climbed only in summer and just for the view. On a clear day, you could see for a distance of four hundred miles.

At last Louis could see for himself the "alps" where sheep and cattle pastured. He clambered up steep trails

to come out on level pastureland, then climbed again and once more crossed fields lush with grass. Great chestnut trees grew here and there as though set out by a master gardener to make a pretty scene. Most of the German students vied with each other, running races up a steep slope and then stopping for a mock wrestling match. Louis was proud of his strength and wrestled with the best of them. But he also stopped to look at almost every rock he saw and he did not care at all if his friends laughed at him. The knapsack that he carried on his back was soon full of stones.

From the summit of the Rigi a great snowy circle of peaks could be seen crowding the whole horizon — the Wetterhorn, the Jungfrau — Louis wished that he could name them all. Very few of the snow-covered peaks had ever been scaled and he felt a great longing to be the first to climb a famous mountain. Of this he said nothing. His German friends, having raced each other to the top of the Rigi, bought food at the little inn on the summit and then stretched out on the ground to fall asleep almost as soon as it was dark.

Agassiz lay awake for hours. He had been watching a thunderstorm gathering over Lake Constance, far below. Lightning leaped from cloud to cloud. The lake was blotted out of sight in rain and yet the sky overhead was clear. It was the first time that Louis had ever watched a storm from above the clouds and it was a sight he would never forget. He watched the storm's journey, marked by lightning, until it disappeared down a far valley and his mind was seething with questions: What makes a storm? Do they always follow valleys? Perhaps high mountain ranges guide the course of storms the way a sheep dog herds his sheep?

"We must go to Heidelberg," Louis told his brother, after they had spent nearly two years at Zurich. The questions constantly coming into Louis's mind were not being answered in a medical college and German students had been telling him about the great Heidelberg University.

"*You* must go," Augustus said. "But I am going home. There is a place for me in the bank at Neuchâtel."

"You think that Father can send only one of us, don't you?" Louis said. "That's why you're going into the bank — just so that I can go on."

"That's partly the reason," admitted Augustus. "But besides that, I don't really think I could ever become a museum director and I don't believe I'd make a very good doctor. I'd really like it in a bank. I'm good at figures and you're not. And I'd have time to help you collect specimens."

All this was true and Louis knew it. It was also true that Augustus would have gone to Heidelberg if there had been money enough for both boys.

When Louis set out on his first journey into a foreign

country, he promised to write to Augustus often. Heidelberg lay almost due north and at least a hundred and eighty miles from the Lake of Neuchâtel. It was an old city on the swift-flowing Neckar River, a few miles from the place where the Neckar joins the much quieter waters of the Rhine. A great castle frowned down upon the town and in the streets students with sabers at their side jostled mere passers-by.

"I get up at six every morning, dress and have breakfast," Louis wrote to his brother. "At seven I go to my lectures given during the morning at the Museum building, which is next to the laboratory for the study of anatomy. From twelve to one, I practice fencing, after which I walk till two, when I return to my room and to my studies till five." Then came the lectures that he liked best. A famous professor compared the bones of different animals with each other and with the bones of man. Comparative anatomy, this was called. Someday Louis Agassiz would be famous for studies in comparative zoology.

Young Agassiz missed his brother, but he found a new friend — Alexander Braun, a student of botany who lived in Karlsruhe, only about thirty miles away. When Alexander wrote home, he said, "I often go on a hunt after animals and plants with the new student named Agassiz. Not only do we collect and learn to observe all manner of things but I have learned a great deal from

Agassiz, who is more at home in zoology than I am. He can recognize the birds from far off by their song and can give a name to every fish in the water. In the morning we often stroll together through the fish market, where he explains to me the different species. He is going to show me how to mount fishes and then we intend to make a collection of all the native kinds."

Louis was now too far away from home to think of going there for vacations. But Alexander Braun invited him to his house, where everyone treated him like a member of the family. Alexander had a brother, Maximilian, and two sisters, Cecile and Emmy. Their father was a botanist, and a room in their house was fitted up with long work tables, with microscopes and with presses for keeping botanical specimens. Cecile studied art and often helped her father and her brothers by making careful drawings of plants and flowers.

"I have a sister of my own named Cecile," Louis told Cecile Braun. "She draws fish for me."

In the spring of 1827, when Louis Agassiz was not quite twenty, he fell ill of a fever. Alexander Braun took him home to Karlsruhe as soon as he was well enough to travel. The Brauns took care of him and Cecile learned to draw fish — just to please him.

For all the Brauns' kindness, Louis could not seem to get his strength back. As soon as he could make the long journey, he went back home to Switzerland. The doctors in his family took a look at his pale cheeks and told him to stay out of doors as much as he could. This was just what he liked best, and soon he was roaming the hills near the Lake of Neuchâtel and collecting all the flowers he could find. He made a list of them — the first that anyone had ever written down.

Louis had not forgotten the lake. It seems strange, but so far no one had really observed how frogs' eggs develop. Louis put lake water into a glass bowl and found some frogs' eggs that had just a tiny black dot in each clear jelly-like drop. His sister Cecile drew a picture each day, showing how the dot grew larger, developed a tail, and then finally swam about as a tadpole. "We'll raise some fine little frogs," he told her, "and I will take them back to my professor of zoology."

But Louis Agassiz did not go back to Heidelberg. "It is a good school for boys learning to become Protestant ministers like you," he explained to his father. "Or if I wanted to be a lawyer, Heidelberg is the place. But for the study of medicine, Heidelberg is old-fashioned."

Alexander Braun was thinking the same thing. The University of Munich would suit both boys better. Some of the leading young professors were there, teaching "popular astronomy, natural history, botany and mineralogy." These subjects did not seem practical to Louis's father but Louis promised to work hard for his medical degree.

Munich is in the southeastern part of Germany not far from the border of Austria. But Louis Agassiz went first to Karlsruhe so that he and Alexander Braun could set out together. Part of the way, the boys rode in a horse-drawn coach called the post. At different places the horses were unharnessed and fresh horses harnessed up so that the coach could be driven at a gallop — "post-haste" — all the way. But when the boys got to Stuttgart, the first large city on their route, they forgot all about haste. There was a natural history museum at Stuttgart.

"I saw many things quite new to me," Louis wrote home to his brother Augustus. There was "a North American buffalo of immense size" and there were "fossil bones of a mammoth." So little was then known about prehistoric animals that Louis needed to explain. "You know that the mammoth is no longer living. Some fishermen, digging recently on the border of the Obi river in Siberia, found one of these animals frozen in a mass of ice, at a depth of sixty feet, so well preserved that it was still covered with hair as in life." When exposed to the air, the flesh dropped away from the bones of this elephant-like creature. But there was a shred of its skin with hair on it displayed at the Museum of Natural History at Stuttgart. It was "as coarse as fine twine and nearly a foot long," Louis said.

Louis Agassiz asked questions about this mammoth.

"But what I should like to know is how this animal could wander so far north and then in what manner it died, to be frozen thus intact and remain intact perhaps for countless ages." The twenty-year-old Agassiz had just stated a problem which still puzzles scientists today. Recently, new explanations have appeared.

The two students called on people interested in natural science, whether they had met them before or not. Louis had some pressed grasses from Switzerland and Alexander had botanical specimens from Bavaria. "We look like peddlers, opening our packs," laughed Louis. But they constantly exchanged their own specimens for something they needed from the scientists they met as they went along. What need of money when a fern or a stalk of marsh grass would do just as well!

The boys visited a Heidelberg classmate and discovered that their friend's father had "a superb collection of fossils" and "quite a large collection of shells from the Adriatic Sea." These were not identified but both Louis and Alexander knew what they were called.

"If you will arrange and label my shells for me," said this man, "I will give you my duplicates." He had more than one of almost everything. Here was another way to earn specimens without spending money and Louis and Alexander set to work. In three hours they did a fine job.

But now time was running out. They must be on their

way if they were to arrive in Munich for the opening of the term, so once more they traveled post-haste. Agassiz's next letter home was from Munich.

"Friday is market day here," he said. "I never miss going to see the fish and to increase my collection." At first he knew the names of all the fish he saw. Then one morning there was a fish that was new to him. He bought it and rushed back to his room. No — there was nothing like it described in any of his notebooks. At the university there were no books describing it and Professor Martius, whose specialty was fish, had never seen one. Louis sat down and wrote a careful description and sent his article to a magazine for natural scientists. It was printed and Louis Agassiz knew the thrill of seeing his own work published for the first time.

There was something still more exciting about this event. Louis had chosen a Latin name for his fish with his own name in Latin at the end. Someday there would be many fish and fossil fish whose names ended with *Agassii*. Sometimes this was shortened to *Agass* or even *Ag* and before long, the name of Agassiz in some form or other would be found in every natural history museum where fish are shown. But this was the first time that Louis had seen his Latin name in print and it was the most exciting time of all. Here was a dream come true. And if one dream can come true, why not many more?

The professor at Munich, whom Louis called "Mon-

sieur de Martius," had just returned from Brazil with "a magnificent collection of insects, shells and fish," as Louis told his brother. Martius now sent for Louis Agassiz. "You know more about fish than any other student here," he said. "As a matter of fact, you know more than any man I have ever met. My colleague Spix, who was to have described our collection of Brazilian fish, is dead and I cannot do the work myself. Will you take it over?"

Young Agassiz was almost overcome by the compliment paid him. He never thought of asking for any money but seized the opportunity to do the kind of work he loved best. His name was to be on the title page. When Louis was fourteen he had planned that he would begin to write when he was twenty-five. He was now only twenty-one and his opportunity to write a book had come. The book was to be written in Latin so that scholars of all nations could read it, but this was no trouble for Louis. He wrote Latin as easily as he did French and German.

The book on Brazilian fishes was almost finished when Professor Martius suggested that Louis Agassiz's name would look better on the title page if it had a degree after it. Agassiz was surprised. Professors in the different schools he had attended had always written letters telling what a good student he was. With these letters he had gone to other professors, taking what courses he needed in order to find out the special things he wanted to know. Then he had gone on in search of teachers who had still more to tell him. But Agassiz said he would be glad to take examinations for a degree if there were any point to it.

Written examinations were given first. After passing these, a student must meet a group of professors and answer their questions aloud and on the spot for hours at a time. Louis Agassiz took the written examinations and his papers were so nearly perfect that it was decided that he did not need to take the oral examinations at all. He was now a doctor of philosophy.

It was a proud moment for Louis when he was able to send his first book to his father. Now the time had come for him to say that he did not want to be a doctor of medicine after all. "I wish it may be said of Louis Agassiz that he was the first naturalist of his time, a good citizen and a good son," he wrote.

The Reverend Mr. Agassiz was "pleased beyond words with the beautiful book." But he still believed that Louis would starve before he ever earned a living as a naturalist. His son had taken the wrong degree and now he must still win a degree in "medicine and surgery." In Switzerland, a son did as his father told him to do. Louis promised to become Louis Agassiz, M.D., as well as Louis Agassiz, Ph.D.

6

On to Paris

LOUIS AGASSIZ had now achieved two of his greatest ambitions. He had discovered a new species of fish and put his name to it and he had written a book. But even before he reached one goal he saw another shining far ahead of him. What he now wanted most was to go on a scientific expedition. He listened eagerly to everything Professor Martius could tell him about Brazil. Someday, somehow, he must go there. He heard that the great geographer Humboldt was going to the Ural Mountains, which stretch from the Arctic Ocean nearly to the Caspian Sea. There was gold in those ranges, and platinum and even diamonds. But what Agassiz wanted to see was a "paleozoic stratum" — a layer of very ancient rock with many fossils. The very thought of going with Humboldt pleased him so that he jumped into a snowbank and rolled in the snow on his way home from a professor's house where he had heard about the expedition. This was partly to express joy but partly to show his friends who were with him how strong and unafraid of cold he was.

Humboldt chose two other young men to go on his expedition. This was a great blow to Louis Agassiz. But instead of giving up hope he began to prepare himself for some other expedition just in case the chance to join one came along.

"I have learned to skin all sorts of animals, even very large ones," Louis said. "I have made more than a hundred skeletons of quadrupeds, birds, reptiles and fish; I have tested all the various ways of preserving such animals as should not be skinned. I have for six months frequented a blacksmith's shop, learning to handle hammer and ax, and I also practice arms, the bayonet and saber exercise. I am strong and robust, know how to swim and do not fear forced marches." During vacations at Munich he often walked "twelve or fifteen leagues a day [about thirty or thirty-five miles] for eight days at a time". on a botany or a geology trip. He carried a knapsack which daily grew heavier with the specimens he collected. Agassiz never had any use for "closet scientists," as he called the people who studied only books without going outdoors to see for themselves what the world of nature was really like.

As soon as his work on Brazilian fish was done, Agassiz's professors at Munich urged him to write about fossil fish. He was the one who knew the most about them, but he would never get credit for this unless he published a book soon. It was also Louis Agassiz who now knew the most about fresh-water fish in Europe and he must get to work on a book about them. Louis took an attic room with Alexander Braun.

All sorts of preparations went on. Fish were boiled slowly in water over a charcoal brazier so that the flesh would fall off and the bones could be studied. Bones of modern fish were compared with bones of fossil fish. Fellow students dropped by to discuss various scientific problems, and if the fish kettle was not in use it would do to boil coffee. No one minded the fishy taste. Botanical specimens belonging to Alexander Braun littered the couch, benches and the floor. Books were piled on chairs. The walls of the room were painted white and soon they were covered with diagrams and notes. There was an art school in Munich and artists dropped by, adding human skeletons and caricatures to the walls.

In the evening, students — and sometimes professors — met in Agassiz's room to take turns giving lectures on their favorite subjects. Lively, sometimes violent discussions followed. "The Little Academy," they called Agassiz's group of friends, and he was their leader.

It is hard to imagine the difficulty of writing a scientific book that must have many pictures — in the days before photographs were used. "I must get hold of someone to do my drawings for me," Agassiz told Alexander Braun.

"My sister could do them," Alexander remarked.

"And so could mine," agreed Agassiz. But both girls lived too far away to be of any help. Then Agassiz re-

membered the art school, where there were students who
could draw wonderfully well and who would be glad to
earn a little money. Word went around that Louis Agassiz was looking for an artist and Joseph Denkel appeared
at the door of Agassiz's attic laboratory.

Joseph was a German boy with a solemn face and
round blue eyes. He had hardly ever looked at a fish except on a dinner plate, but Agassiz told him to make
"colored drawings of fishes from life."

"We walked to a place out of town where fish were
kept," Denkel said. "I made a colored drawing of a richly
colored trout with many fine colored spots, he pointing
out to me the features to be well done." Joseph had no
idea that Agassiz's enthusiasm was contagious — until he
had caught it. "We both became very friendly to each
other," he said in his German way. "I found myself almost daily three or four hours with him engaged with
painting fresh-water fish from life. He was at my side,
partly writing his descriptions, partly giving me infor-
mation about fish."

Of course Agassiz had almost no money. What he had
he kept in a little compartment in the chest where his
clothes were and Denkel was free to help himself. The
German boy never took any more than a very little pay
and he worked for Agassiz for years doing beautiful
drawings. His fish skeletons seemed to stand out from
the page, the lines fine, smooth, with never a mistake.

He drew bony heads with jaws that seemed ready to open.

Agassiz had not forgotten his promise to his father about that medical and surgical degree. He outlined a plan of study for himself and found a classmate who would work with him evenings. Every night they read aloud to each other, one night from a German medical book and the next night from one in French. When the reading was over, each gave the other a test, asking questions to make sure that everything they read they understood and remembered. This left Agassiz free to work all day on his own books.

There were no games which students played together at Munich, such as football or baseball. Fencing was the sport, and it required strength, skill and practice. Agassiz never became weak and pale from working too hard because he always took time for fencing every day. There were places to go for practice and for fencing bouts the way there are roller-skating rinks and bowling alleys today. And there was an art student who had learned to fence left-handed for fear of injuring his painting hand. This gave him an advantage and he won all his bouts. But Agassiz practiced secretly until he too could fence with his left hand. Then he challenged the artist to a bout and their friends gathered. They were surprised when Agassiz won — but Louis was not. Whatever he set out to do he did well. He fenced German-style with a heavy saber rather than a French foil, and all he learned he taught himself because he could not afford fencing masters.

In April 1830, just before he was twenty-three years old, Louis Agassiz passed his medical examinations. The examinations lasted nine days and he was very much praised for his answers to the many questions, both written and oral.

A publisher began work on the first volume of Agassiz's book about fossil fish. When it was done, there would be five volumes and it would be easy to read. Agassiz told about the fossils he had found and he told where other people had found some. His own enthusiasm made his book interesting not only to scientists but to anyone who liked fossils and had collections of them.

Now Agassiz packed up his own collection of fossil fish, his glass jars of fish preserved in alcohol, his pressed flowers and leaves, his insects and his animal and bird specimens. He was going home to Switzerland after more than ten years of study. He stopped first in Lausanne to see his uncle Dr. Mathias Mayor.

With great pride Dr. Mayor introduced his nephew to his friends everywhere as "Monsieur le Docteur Agassiz." He took Louis to the hospital to observe an operation. Surely there would be a place at the hospital for a young man who had passed his medical examinations so brilliantly. But at this time ether had not yet been discovered, and the patient was usually strapped to the operating table to suffer terrible pain. The operation that Louis was to observe had hardly begun when young Dr. Agassiz fainted.

Louis was by no means the first or the last young doctor to faint when he watched an operation, Dr. Mayor assured him. Many fine surgeons fainted again and again before grim determination won out. Dr. Mayor was not at all discouraged.

But now uncle and nephew had a long talk. Louis showed some of the work he had done, not only for his book on fossil fish but on the next one, *The Natural History of Fresh-Water Fish of Central Europe*. Dr. Mayor had many friends who were natural scientists and he could see that Louis loved natural history with his whole heart. There was no use in asking him to go into medicine just because he would be able to learn all that a doctor should know. A boy might have trouble with his medical studies and still make a better doctor. For the first time, Louis had someone on his side in his family.

"I cannot thank you enough, dear Louis, for the happiness you have given me in completing your medical examination," his mother had written. Now he had "a safe career," she said. So Louis Agassiz went home to Orbe, on Lake Neuchâtel. He actually tried to practice medicine for a little while, but his mother soon saw that he was not happy. Her brother and other relatives offered to lend money so that Louis could go to Paris to study collections of fossils there and complete his book.

The journey to Paris was the longest Louis Agassiz had ever made. Paris was the largest city he had ever seen and it was a beautiful one. But Agassiz paid no attention to the famous opera, art collections or historic Notre Dame Cathedral. He went straight to the Left Bank of the Seine where students lived and took a small room close to the Jardin des Plantes, which was to him the most important place in Paris.

Louis went at once to call on the Baron de Cuvier, known as "the first scientist in Europe," but he went with a heavy heart. Just before leaving home he had heard that Cuvier was writing a book on fossil fish. If so, who would read one on the same subject by an unknown young man named Agassiz!

Louis tucked a huge portfolio of drawings under his arm and set out for the Baron's house. Cuvier was a little cold and distant, Louis thought. They talked and Louis showed his work. Then he went away and heard nothing from the Baron for nearly a week.

At last a message came. Would young Dr. Agassiz spend Saturday with the Baron de Cuvier? Indeed he would! Louis arrived early and this time the Baron sent his secretary for notes and specimens. "You are in this field ahead of me," he told Agassiz. "If I were young

again, we might work together." And this was all that
Louis had really hoped for — that he might be allowed
to help the Baron.

"I will give you these notes," said Cuvier. "You may
use my specimens and I want you to work here at my
house. The subject is yours and you alone shall write the
book."

This was the most generous gift that Agassiz could
have received — the work of another scientist. Usually
he knew just what to say, but now he could hardly speak,
he was so happy. But the Baron understood. Agassiz
"worked at least fifteen hours a day" at Baron Cuvier's
house.

About a year after Agassiz and the Baron de Cuvier
met, Cuvier died. Agassiz had arrived in Paris just in
time to receive the gift of Cuvier's work. But Cuvier had
promised to help Agassiz to find people who would buy
his book after it was published and it was a pity that this
promise could not be kept.

Agassiz had already met Baron von Humboldt, another of his heroes in the scientific world. Humboldt was
a mineralogist, botanist and astronomer. He used his
knowledge of astronomy to make maps and he corrected
a mistake of as much as three hundred miles in the posi-
tion of Mexico on the maps of his time. Young Agassiz
told Humboldt how much he admired him and there was
no better way of making friends.

But by this time, the money that Agassiz had borrowed from his family was almost gone. His mother wrote to him: "Stop living on bright dreams. Come home and give lessons."

Louis gave up hope of ever finishing his book with all its fine pictures. When he started writing about fossil fish he had discovered five hundred different kinds. He knew that there were fossil fish in collections in England which he had never seen. There must be others all over the world. And Louis Agassiz had at most only a week longer to work on his book!

7

Famous Naturalist

EARLY EVERY MORNING, Louis Agassiz crossed a paved court to an old building at the Jardin des Plantes in Paris. The building was so rickety that it had to be propped up with timbers on the outside. But inside was one of the world's finest fossil collections. They were heaped on dusty shelves, most of them unmarked because almost no one knew anything about them.

A brown painted door had a bell rope hanging beside it. Under the rope was a sign which said in French, "Pull hard." The caretaker, who was deaf, always recognized the loud jangle the bell gave when Louis Agassiz pulled that rope. He would hurry to the door, for he loved Louis's bright smile and cheery good morning. Years later, when people came to see the place where the famous naturalist once worked, the caretaker would point out a pine table on an upper floor. He would call attention to labels in neat handwriting which Agassiz had made to help future students.

Everyone noticed when Agassiz's bright smile was gone. They asked why he was suddenly so sad and he explained that he must soon give up the work he loved. It was about this time that Baron von Humboldt called on Agassiz at his dreary little hotel, number 4 Rue Copeau, just outside the Jardin des Plantes. He prowled around Agassiz's small room up under the roof and looked at the books Agassiz owned. There were very few indeed that had been written by Humboldt. A whole collection of Humboldt's books would have cost about two thousand dollars. But Humboldt immediately noticed the books made out of scraps of paper sewed together. Here he found all the most important parts of his own work carefully copied out by Agassiz and his brother, years ago at Lausanne. The Baron could not help feeling pleased.

Baron von Humboldt was a wealthy man and he loved the study of science. He could buy all the books he wanted, go on expeditions and hire assistants to go with him. But he could also imagine how it would feel to be a student with almost no money at all. He invited Agassiz to dinner at one of the best restaurants in Paris. Agassiz had often looked through the windows at this famous place but had never dreamed that he would go inside. Humboldt ordered soup and oysters, beef with a special sauce, then pheasant, then cakes and custards. The meal lasted for three hours. While they ate, Humboldt asked questions to find out if young Agassiz really knew much about natural science.

"How he examined me!" said Agassiz afterwards. "And how much I learned!"

The Baron von Humboldt himself might have said,

"How the young man ate!" Agassiz always had a big appetite and he had been trying for a long time to save money by eating very little.

Agassiz made all his plans to leave Paris. It was almost his last day, and he sat in an iron chair in the courtyard in front of the hotel — hungry as usual. He thought he would rest a while and then take a last look at the fossils. A servant in a handsome dark red uniform came into the court and looked around with his nose in the air. "Can

you tell me where to find Monsieur le Docteur Agassiz?" the man inquired.

"That's my name," said Agassiz and the servant handed him a letter.

"There's no reply," he said.

Agassiz opened the letter, which was from Humboldt. "A man so gifted as you are should be able to continue his work," the Baron wrote. He realized that Louis Agassiz was proud and might not feel he could accept any help from anyone outside his family. But he enclosed money "as a loan that need not be repaid." It was such a friendly letter that Agassiz accepted the loan.

Work on the fossils in Paris lasted four or five months longer and then Agassiz took a vacation. Alexander Braun was in Paris, studying botany, and Denkel was there, helping Agassiz. The three young men set out for the coast of Normandy. The distance was only a little over a hundred miles, so of course they walked! They carried knapsacks on their backs and they slept under the stars or in some friendly farmer's barn if it rained. They bought bread and cheese to eat by the roadside and now and then they had a fine filling meal at a country inn. Sometimes they got a lift in a farmer's cart but as a rule the young scientists preferred to be on foot. Alexander collected flowers and grasses, Denkel made a sketch or two when a scene pleased him, and Louis Agassiz wanted a rock specimen from every rocky outcropping he saw.

One morning early there was a new scent in the air. It was not the apple blossoms for which Normandy was famous. It was the smell of salt and seaweed. Houses on top of a little hill had a shining look as though they reflected something bright beyond them. The three friends topped the rise and there it was! "The sea, the far-sounding sea!" shouted Agassiz. Now he knew exactly how the Greek soldiers felt as they caught sight of the sea after a long march. He remembered how he had stood in front of his father's desk reciting the story of the Greek general Xenophon. Now he too was looking at the sea and it was true that there was no land in sight. The water met the sky in a far horizon and on Louis Agassiz's face was the look his friends called "radiant."

"At last I have looked upon the sea and all its riches," Louis wrote home to his brother Augustus. He tried to catch all the fish he possibly could in the short time he could stay on the Normandy coast. And there were other "riches" in the form of jellyfish, starfish and snails. Sea anemones, which looked like flowers but were really sea animals, fascinated Agassiz. The sea was full of life and a whole new world of discovery opened before him. Someday, he told himself, he would study everything in it, from sea worms to whales.

The vacation ended as even the best of vacations do. Now it was Augustus who wrote to Louis of a wonderful chance back home. Augustus was living in Neuchâtel, where there was a sort of junior college and a natural history museum. The museum had nothing much in it and no director. At the college there was no one to teach natural science. Here was just the place for Louis, and Augustus knew of a wealthy man in Neuchâtel whose hobby was natural science and who might help out in the matter of salary.

Agassiz accepted the job. He never asked about money and it made no difference to him when he found that he would get only about three hundred dollars a year for teaching some hundred students and for looking after the museum. There would be time for him to go on with his own work and this was much more important to him than a large salary. It would be good to see Augustus again. They could make collections together. Near Neuchâtel was a broad streak of limestone filled with the fossil remains of prehistoric turtles and huge fish. Agassiz had heard about them at Lausanne for the first time and now he could collect wonderful specimens and have time to study them. The age in prehistoric time when giant reptiles roamed the earth is now called Jurassic because of this streak of limestone running through the Jura Mountains. Louis Agassiz was the pioneer in the study of the Jurassic period.

Baron von Humboldt was disappointed when Agassiz went to Neuchâtel to teach in a little college nobody ever heard of. Agassiz had been asked to teach at Heidelberg and Humboldt begged him at least to tell everyone about the honor. Here was a young man who put his work first and cared very little about a high salary. Humboldt could not help liking Agassiz for this very reason and he tried to help in another way. Neuchâtel, although in Switzerland, belonged to the kingdom of Prussia. Humboldt told King Friedrich Wilhelm III about Agassiz.

The collection that Agassiz had been making ever since he was a boy was now very large. It was also hard to take care of and expensive — because the preserving alcohol was forever leaking out of the glass jars and having to be renewed. But here was the city of Neuchâtel where there was a museum in need of specimens. A subscription was raised to buy Agassiz's collection and the King of Prussia himself headed the list. Agassiz received about three thousand dollars.

In the autumn of 1833, Agassiz went to Karlsruhe to visit the Brauns. This time it was not Alexander he most wanted to see, but Alexander's sister Cecile. They had met first when she was seventeen and he was not quite twenty. Perhaps they soon fell in love but Agassiz had no money. Now he had a job and he and Cecile were married.

The young Agassiz couple found a place to live in Neuchâtel. Cecile was happy to be able to draw so well that many of her illustrations were published in her husband's books. Perhaps Denkel's fossils were the best but Cecile's fish drawn from life actually looked lively. When the five-volume work on fossil fish was ready at last, Agassiz received the Wollaston Prize of over a hundred and fifty dollars.

Agassiz never tried to become famous, but Humboldt need not have worried. Fame had now come to Agassiz whether he wanted it or not. He was the leading ichthyologist in all Europe, and instead of being forgotten in the little city of Neuchâtel he made that city famous. People from the whole continent of Europe came to consult with him. Tourists asked to have him pointed out to them on the streets.

It was easy enough to point out Agassiz because he usually had a crowd of children following him. There was nothing he loved more than to tell children all about the wonderful things in the world of nature. He was never too busy to talk to them. Boys and girls helped him a great deal in his fossil collecting, for they had sharp eyes and soon learned what to look for.

The regular college students came to Agassiz's lectures of course. But soon the townspeople heard how interesting the lectures were and they came too. Even today the city of Neuchâtel is a favorite gathering place for natural scientists and its Natural History Museum is mentioned in all the guidebooks.

Although Louis Agassiz's specialty was fish, he was

always interested in everything he saw. He had not forgotten his own unanswered questions about strange boulders like the one used for a fish-pool when he was a boy. He was still working on his books on fish when he began to wonder what had moved the great rocks. Could it have been ice?

"Don't bother with such absurd ideas," warned Humboldt in a letter to Agassiz. "Keep on with the work which is making you famous."

8

Adventures in the Alps

GREAT FROZEN RIVERS covered with snow lay in the alpine valleys just below the snow-covered peaks. They were called glaciers. Louis Agassiz had never seen a glacier except at a distance. He lived among practical, hardworking Swiss people and there was no good reason for climbing a glacier — so far as anyone knew. In Switzerland there was still no such thing as winter sports and only a few people were beginning to try to scale alpine peaks.

But in 1836, Agassiz went to a town called Bex in the valley of the Rhone. His scientist friend Charpentier, whom he had met at Lausanne, had just told him about great boulders near Bex that might have been brought there by a glacier that had since melted. When Agassiz looked at them he thought so too. And here at last was a reason for studying glaciers and trying to learn just what a great river of ice could do.

Agassiz visited all the greatest glaciers in Switzerland, those just below the summit of Mont Blanc being the most impressive. People said that glaciers did not move — they just melted at the lower end, forming a mountain stream. By setting stakes in the ice and others on the mountainside opposite, Agassiz proved that the ice itself

moved, carrying one set of stakes downward. Movement
of a glacier was too slow to see just by looking at it. The
ice was so powerful that it carried rocks on its back
which a river could not have moved. Broken rocks that
stayed on top of the ice had jagged edges, but rocks
caught underneath the ice were rolled and ground until
they were smooth.

Now Agassiz's imagination took a tremendous leap.
Suppose there had been glaciers in different places all
over the earth? Suppose there had been an "ice age"? It
seems strange today that there was a time when people
did not know about the "glacial theory." But when Louis
Agassiz wrote a paper telling of this idea, almost everyone laughed at him. This was when his old friend Baron
von Humboldt told him to go back to his fish and not
talk nonsense.

The idea of an ice age had taken hold of Agassiz's mind
and he could not let it go. The Jungfrau had always been
his favorite mountain and he chose the Aar glacier, not
very far from the Jungfrau, for his glacial studies. The
first summer, he took four assistants and a student named
Pourtalès with him into the Aar valley. They brought
along a great many scientific instruments as well as food,
blankets, kettles and a frying pan. Among the rocks being carried slowly down the valley by the glacier there
was a huge boulder with an overhanging slab of rock at
the top. Here was almost a cave. Other rocks were lying

around and the men piled them up to make two more walls. Then they slung a blanket across the front.

All day long Agassiz and his friends worked, measuring, drawing diagrams, collecting specimens of rock that had been polished or grooved by ice. At night they built a big fire in front of their rock shelter. The food they cooked tasted wonderfully good and they sang songs and told stories around their campfire.

Agassiz always got acquainted with everyone wherever he went. There was a small village on the Aar River where he found two men living who had acted as guides for one of the earliest mountain climbers in Switzerland. He hired these men to join his party on the glacier.

At last the work was finished and Agassiz had promised his men a little fun. They would climb through a high defile and then go down on the other side into another valley. It was Agassiz's young student, seventeen years old, who told about it. "We waded knee-deep in fresh snow," Pourtalès said. "When we got close to the summit of 'Strahligg' we roped ourselves together." Now the guides went ahead and cut steps in the ice. No one, so far as they knew, had ever been into the Strahligg pass before. When they reached the top of the pass they were surprised to find "a small plateau." The snow was fresh and soft. Everyone was so excited that "the guides began to wrestle and we to dance," said Pourtalès.

On the way down the far side of the mountain they

came to another glacier. There was a crevasse in the ice twenty feet wide and so deep it seemed to have no bottom. Here they might have had to turn back, but there was "a bridge of ice, one or two feet wide." They crossed it. But the bridge was broken off toward the end. They "were obliged to spring across" this last terrifying gap, as Pourtalès would always remember.

People in the valley below could hardly believe their eyes when Agassiz and his friends came down the mountain. "How did you get here!" they exclaimed. "No one can cross the Strahligg pass!"

The following summer Agassiz went back to his camp on the glacier. Now he was determined to find out what it was like *inside* the river of ice. Large holes in the ice were a common sight. They were called "wells" and Agassiz determined to go down into one. He fixed a tripod over a well. A rope was fastened to it and a big loop tied in the rope and then a wooden seat was fastened into the loop. Agassiz sat on the seat the way he used to do in a rope swing in the garden when he was a boy. Now his assistants lowered away. One of them lay flat on the ice with his head over the hole "to listen for a warning cry" and a series of signals were agreed upon.

Agassiz had himself lowered eighty feet. Here he found that the well divided into two parts. Signaling by pulling on the rope, he had himself raised a little and then lowered into one of the two holes in the ice. This divided

again — Agassiz chose a new shaft and went on down. He was counting bands of blue or white ice and having a wonderful time.

Now he was a hundred and twenty feet down. And suddenly he was plunged into ice water. There was a deep, fast-flowing river under the ice. Agassiz tugged at the rope, but the men up on top misunderstood the signal and lowered away. A "warning cry" could not be heard.

Agassiz managed to make a clear signal and now his swing-seat began to rise. But he saw that all around him were "mammoth icicles" that threatened to cut the rope. Somehow he "steered around them" and reached the top of the glacier. He gave a joyful shout when he was safe at last. He said he would not have gone down into the well if he had known how dangerous it would be. But he published an article on "glacial bands" which was of great interest to fellow scientists.

These summers of hard work were vacations to Agassiz. In winter he taught his classes, worked on his books and gave lectures. He enjoyed all this but he always looked forward to summer in the Alps. He took his family along to enjoy a vacation too and they lived in a mountain chalet far above the floor of the valley but below the snow and ice.

Agassiz now had three children. Alexander, the oldest, was named for his uncle Alexander Braun. Then came

Ida, whose name was always pronounced "Eeda," and then there was Pauline. The children loved the mountains and Alex was always begging his father to take him up on the glacier. His father promised and at last the day came.

Alex waved good-by to his sisters and set out with the men up the steep mountain trail. Before long the trail led over rocks that were too high for Alex. He was only six years old and although his courage was high, his legs were short. But Jacob, the guide who worked for Agassiz every summer, had provided for this emergency. He had a big basket on his back and when the going got too rough he put Alex in the basket.

Afterwards Mr. Burkhardt, an artist working with Agassiz, drew a picture showing the party climbing over the steep rocks toward the cave. He drew the guide with the big basket and Alex was very proud. Of course he was inside where no one could see him but he considered this a picture of himself just the same.

At the end of summer came the reward for hard work. This time, Agassiz made up a party of eleven people to climb the Jungfrau. About nine years before, one of the earliest alpine climbers had attempted the Jungfrau and failed. The peak was considered "unscalable." But to climb it had always been Louis Agassiz's dream and he was sure he could do it.

The guides who were with the first climbers in their

unsuccessful attempt were the ones who had been working for Agassiz for several years. Jacob was their leader
and he was eager to go with Agassiz to try again. He
chose five men to help him — to cut steps in the ice, to
carry ropes and equipment. Borrowing Agassiz's powerful binoculars, Jacob studied the slopes of the Jungfrau,

which rose to a narrow summit almost as pointed as the
spire of a church. There was a steep cliff at the top, and
up the cliff must go not only the climbers but their
barometer so that the height of the peak could be measured. In Agassiz's time it was a new idea to measure
height by barometric pressure,

At last the great day came. Starting early in the morning, the party climbed to a little inn near the top of the pass in the Bernese Alps nearest the Jungfrau. Here they spent the night and started out at four next morning. They climbed all day, reaching and crossing a high plateau. The snow seemed solid beneath them but Agassiz noticed curious window-like openings. Stooping down to look into one, he saw a great cave of ice filled with blue light. It was a beautiful sight but at the same time terrifying. They were walking on a crust over a huge crevasse and there was no telling how thick the crust of ice and snow might be.

They roped themselves together and traveled single file, so that if the leader went through the crust, the others could pull him back. They moved as fast as they could and the crust held. Another night was spent at a group of three or four chalets — the highest houses on the shoulder of the Jungfrau.

Jacob had made a ladder which he had used in the unsuccessful attempt to scale the Jungfrau. He had left it at these chalets and he expected to find it there to use again. But the ladder was gone. Two of the guides spent most of the night climbing down to the nearest village to find who had taken it. Agassiz meant to set out at three the next morning but it was five before the ladder was found and brought up to the high chalets. Now they would have to make forced marches if they hoped to reach the summit and return before dark.

Agassiz and his party pushed forward over steep rocks without a rest until noon. They reached a tiny lake, just under the sharp-pointed summit. There were chunks of ice floating in the lake like miniature icebergs.

There was one more brief rest for the climbers in a shallow valley surrounded by high peaks. Here they left everything except the ladder, axes, ropes, the barometer and a little bread and wine. Now they could see that the final stages of the summit rose in a series of ice-covered rock walls. At the top of each successive cliff was a narrow terrace.

They pressed forward and at the foot of the first of the cliffs they found a crevasse. There was no telling how deep it was but the ladder, which was twenty feet long, reached across it and they crawled over, using the ladder for a bridge. Now came the wall of ice. Jacob and another guide cut steps. Then they hauled the ladder up to use as a sort of handrail. Everyone waited on this terrace for Jacob to cut more steps in the next ice-covered wall of rock. While they waited, someone drove an alpenstock into the snow on the edge of the terrace. It went down so easily that it was hastily pulled back and through the hole they could look straight down for thousands of feet! They were standing on overhanging ice and snow.

The day had been clear but now clouds gathered. Every step had to be cut in ice until at last they came to the topmost point of rock. And here the last of the series of rock walls was so steep that even Agassiz said, "We can never make it." Then Jacob threw aside everything he had been carrying, reached as high as he could and hooked his alpenstock into a crevice in the rock. He pulled himself up, gaining a kneehold, then a toehold. He was on the summit! But the summit of the Jungfrau was so sharp that only one person could stand on it at a time.

Next Louis Agassiz, taller than his guide and as strong, pulled himself up to the pinnacle. The clouds moved away, covering a nearby peak and leaving the Jungfrau clear. Matterhorn, Mont Blanc — practically all the famous peaks were in sight. Agassiz had always known that from the Jungfrau he would have one of the most beautiful views in Switzerland. Far to the northeast there were spots of brightness. They were lakes and he knew that one must be Neuchâtel and another Morat.

It was four in the afternoon when Agassiz and his party began the descent. One by one, each had stood on the summit of the Jungfrau and now they were so elated by their success that Jacob had to warn them. "Go slowly. Take it easy," he kept saying. Sometimes it is much more dangerous to come down a mountain than to climb it. But in two hours they covered a distance that

had taken them six hours to climb. It grew dark but
they kept on, passing the place where the crevasses were
most dangerous. Finally the moon rose. And now they
heard a distant yodel which they joyfully answered.
It was a herdsman who had promised to come to meet
them.

The herdsman had a bucket of fresh milk, and when
they found him at the lake where the icebergs were, they
all gathered around. They drank all the milk he had
brought and it seemed as though nothing had ever tasted
so good before. Then on they went to the chalets where
they had spent the night. They arrived half an hour be-

fore midnight and now nothing had ever seemed so good to them as their beds.

People spoke of Agassiz's "famous ascent of the Jung-frau," but he was much more famous for his lectures and writings on the ice age. He told what the world was like in prehistoric times. "The surface of Europe, cov-ered before by tropical plants and inhabited by troops of big elephants and enormous hippopotami and great meat-eating animals, was suddenly buried under a vast mantle of ice, covering alike plains, lakes, seas and pla-teaus. Upon the life and movement of creation fell the silence of death. Springs paused, rivers ceased to flow, and the rays of the sun rising upon this frozen shore (if indeed the sun reached it) were met only by the breath of winter from the north and thunders of crevasses as they opened across the surface of this icy sea."

Today the bones of the huge creatures that Agassiz was talking about can be seen in museums. Pictures drawn by scientists show what the world looked like before the ice age, during the ice age and afterwards. Louis Agassiz never had the chance we have to study these things. He learned about them from the ice and the fossils in his own country. More than anyone else, he was the man who started people thinking about the world in the days before history was written. He was the man who gave the great natural history museums their start, especially in the United States.

So far, Agassiz had been outside his own small country only a few times. He had studied in France and Germany. He had even been to England and Ireland, where people at first refused to believe his glacial theory. But he had found proof, especially in Scotland, that prehistoric ice had been at work. British scientists finally agreed with him. What Agassiz wanted now was to cross the Atlantic Ocean.

9

To America

"I DREAM of making a journey to America," Louis Agassiz said. He wanted to see if there were rocks with scratches on them as though some giant cat had clawed them. These would be called "striated." He wanted to look for boulders scattered here and there in some valley but unlike any nearby rock ledge. They would be called "erratic." The idea of going to America remained nothing but a dream, however, until 1845, when Louis Agassiz was given money by the King of Prussia. With this grant he was to look for glacial evidences in the New World.

Agassiz had the spirit of a pioneer. The chance to see new places and do a new kind of work always seemed to him like a wonderful vacation. But this time he could not take his family with him. Cecile was not well and she had gone back to northern Germany, where she hoped her cough would disappear and her strength return. The little girls went with her. Alex was to stay in Neuchâtel until his school term was over and then follow his mother and his sisters. At the age of twelve, he became the man of the family while his father was away.

Agassiz said good-by to all his friends. Then he got up

very early one morning and went to the inn. The coach, with its galloping horses, left the inn at Neuchâtel at 2 A.M. — long before dawn. Agassiz could not help feeling a little lonely as he waited in the dark street. Then he heard voices singing and the sound of people marching. Around the corner came flaring lights. Agassiz's students at the College of Neuchâtel had formed a torchlight procession to give him a send-off. They gathered in front of the inn, singing and shouting. Speeches were made and it is doubtful if anyone in the neighborhood slept any more that night.

Agassiz went first to Karlsruhe to say good-by to his wife and daughters. He stopped off in Paris, where he bought a fine broad-brimmed black hat and black clothes such as Frenchmen wore. These styles would look strange in America but Agassiz did not know that. Probably he would have worn clothes like that anyway just because he liked them. He was tall and unusually handsome with fine broad shoulders and a wonderfully friendly smile. People were apt to stare at him wherever he went but he paid no attention. He just smiled and made friends everywhere.

In London, Agassiz made a short visit. He lectured on his glacial theory and more and more people came over to his way of thinking. There was one great British scientist who held out against Agassiz. This was Charles Darwin.

Darwin believed that the ancient cave men looked very much like gorillas and were descended from them. He had never seen any gorillas alive but travelers had told about them. As for there being an ice age — Darwin thought not. And Agassiz, although perfectly sure that there had been an ice age, thought that man had always been man and had nothing to do with other animals. In the end, Darwin and Agassiz accepted each other's ideas. But they were never really friends.

While he was in London, Agassiz was invited to watch some fellow scientists who were going to dissect a crocodile. He was very much interested and perfectly delighted when they gave him parts of the crocodile to keep. Ever since he had sold his first collection he had been working on another which he was taking to the United States with him. He must now buy another glass jar and some preserving alcohol, but meanwhile he wrapped up the pieces of crocodile in his handkerchief. Then, carrying this package, he set out along the street in London with an English friend.

This friend, an amateur natural scientist and quite elegantly dressed, eyed Agassiz's bundle. "Don't you think we might take a cab?" he suggested.

"Oh no," said Agassiz, letting all the horse-drawn cabs go clip-clopping by. "I love to walk."

"Well — er — shall we have my servant carry your

package?" persisted the Englishman. Agassiz said it wasn't heavy.

At last Agassiz noticed that people were staring at him and his bundle and that the young Englishman was getting quite red in the face. He remembered that in England gentlemen never carried packages of any kind. There were always people eager to earn a penny or two by carrying things. "Maybe a cab would be a good idea," said Agassiz, trying not to laugh. But now the young man had realized that a scientist could carry any sort of specimen in any way he pleased. In America, Agassiz would find that people were apt to be proud of doing things themselves.

It was the first week in October, 1846, when Louis Agassiz reached Boston, Massachusetts. There were fewer carriages, fewer servants than in London. Boston was a much smaller city. But it looked a little like London with its narrow streets with brick houses set close to the sidewalk. He was surprised to see no beggars holding out their hands for pennies. This was a sight he was used to in Europe and especially in London.

A wide grassy park with tall trees was called Boston Common, they told Agassiz. Beyond the Common was a Botanic Garden, and in the corner of it was a large building built for a circus but now filled with plants, birds and snakes. Agassiz promptly made friends with the men who had started this garden. At this time, the study of natural science was hardly more than a hobby for a few people. Louis Agassiz would soon see that it became much more important.

Agassiz had promised to give some lectures in Boston but they did not start until December. He had part of October and all of November to do as he pleased. What he wanted was to see as much as possible of the country because he thought he would soon have to go back to Switzerland. A railroad had just been built from Boston by way of Springfield, Massachusetts, to New Haven, Connecticut. At New Haven, people took a steamboat that went on Long Island Sound to New York. A trip which now would take only a few hours usually lasted about two days.

But Agassiz was impressed by the train. "The speed is frightful to those not used to it," he said. He remembered the lumbering horse-drawn coaches which climbed the mountain roads in his native Switzerland. Passengers often got out and walked up the hills to lighten the coach-load for the horses. Agassiz thought that Americans hurried too much. This was because of the "irresistible power of steam, carrying such heavy masses along with the swiftness of lightning." But he thought he would soon become just like an American, "impatient of the slightest delay."

"What a country this is!" exclaimed Agassiz. "All

along the railroad between Boston and Springfield are ancient moraines and polished rock." Agassiz called on all the American natural scientists he could find. Not all of them realized that evidences of an ice age were almost everywhere in New England. "I have had the pleasure of converting several of the most distinguished American geologists to my way of thinking," Agassiz said.

Workmen, grading small hills to make the railroad track level, had cut into the earth. These fresh cuts were Agassiz's delight because they laid bare the layers of smooth, rounded pebbles and gravel. Dark granite ledges could be seen with stripes of white quartz all twisted from volcanic fire in prehistoric days. There were layers of sandstone of different colors from gray to reddish brown and Agassiz knew that these had been heaved up from an ocean bed. Everything had a story to tell him about how the earth was made thousands of years ago.

Today workmen have cut and blasted through the hills to make new highways. The earth and rocks are laid bare, ready to tell their story. But if Agassiz lived today he would surely have more to say about "the speed of lightning." Most Americans take no time to stop and look at sandstone to see if there are any fossils in it. But people who are really interested can find them still.

At Hartford, Agassiz saw the Connecticut River and it reminded him of the Rhine between Karlsruhe and

Heidelberg. The rock along the shore was the same, he said. There were "polished rocks everywhere and magnificent furrows in the sandstone."

In New Haven, Agassiz visited Professor Benjamin Silliman of Yale, who had a fine collection of minerals. Then he took the steamboat for New York. "We constantly disturbed numbers of aquatic birds," said Agassiz. "I have never seen such flocks of ducks and gulls."

Agassiz had a cousin in New York who owned a shop where he sold Swiss watches. Cousin Augustus Mayor was not in the least interested in natural history — but this was before Louis Agassiz came to see him. Agassiz had not been in New York very long before Mr. Mayor found himself getting up early every morning and going down to the Fulton Fish Market. Many of these fish were new to Agassiz and he and his cousin filled a big basket with them. Agassiz's contagious enthusiasm made the Fulton Fish Market a wonderful place.

"In five days I had filled a great barrel with different kinds of fish and fresh-water turtles," Agassiz said. He dissected several turtles and "made skeletons" of various fish.

Agassiz made a quick trip to Washington, to Baltimore and to Philadelphia. He went to Princeton to see "electrical apparatus" which was being developed there. But what he really wanted in Princeton was "a rare kind of turtle which could be found in the ditches near the town." It was "remarkable for the form of its jaws and the length of its tail," Agassiz said. He was bitterly disappointed not to catch one. They had all "withdrawn into their winter quarters" and he would have to try again in spring.

All too soon, it was time for Agassiz to return to Boston to begin his lectures. He had set out on this trip with just a carpetbag in his hand. But everywhere he went, people had given him specimens. Never had he met such generous scientists as the Americans, he said. Now he had fossils from Connecticut sandstone, given him at Yale, shells from rivers and lakes given him by scientists in Philadelphia and Washington. And of course there was his own barrel of fish and turtles from New York.

A carpetbag was a fashionable kind of hand luggage with two looped handles. It was made out of carpeting all brightly patterned with red and pink roses or other gay designs. It would be a good place to carry fish skeletons and some of the more fragile shells. But Agassiz acquired a hatbox, more barrels and a packing-case.

At every stop on the railroad, Agassiz hurried to the baggage car to look after his treasures. "You would cry out in dismay if you saw your baggage flung about pellmell like logs of wood," he wrote to friends back in Europe. "If here and there something goes to pieces, no one is astonished. Never mind! We go fast! We gain time! That is what counts."

When Agassiz "cried out" he spoke with a strong foreign accent. As he tried to explain what was in his precious barrels and boxes, people crowded around. He talked to everyone and there was always someone in the crowd who collected specimens of one sort or another. Everyone tried to help and people with collections took down Agassiz's name and Boston address. They promised to send him all sorts of things.

Although this first journey in the United States had been a short one, when Louis Agassiz got back to Boston a great many people had heard of him. He had made friends among scientists and among hobbyists. His lectures were now to make him famous in America the way his books had brought him fame in Europe.

10

Something to Shout About

WHEN AGASSIZ FIRST CAME to the United States, most of the boys in college spent the greater part of their time studying Latin and Greek. Girls were given lessons at home in music, French and fancy needlework. Sometimes they studied Latin just to prove they could keep up with their brothers. It did them very little good because there were only two or three colleges a girl could go to. Only a few people studied natural science, so when Agassiz began to give his lectures on natural history a great deal of what he told was news to almost everybody. He had a wonderfully interesting way of talking. And he drew pictures on a blackboard as he went along.

Those who went to Agassiz's first lecture told all their friends how good it was. Such a big crowd came to the next lecture that many could not even get into the lecture hall. Agassiz agreed to give each talk twice. He spoke at Tremont Temple, which had once been a theater and which held five thousand people.

"Lecture by Agassiz!" shouted the newsboys on the streets of Boston. People rushed around to Tremont Temple to buy tickets. In New York, they heard about the Agassiz lectures and begged him to come to speak. He was offered fourteen hundred dollars for a series of talks. A great many people wanted to learn about the world around them, and Louis Agassiz could tell about it in such an interesting way that he was soon earning more money than he had ever had in his life before. He needed it because a printing press which he had established back in Neuchâtel had failed and had been sold at auction. Agassiz had borrowed money from his family and his friends and had been very unhappy because he could not pay his debts. But now he sent money back to Switzerland and knew that the time would come when all his debts would be paid.

Agassiz had expected to go home to Switzerland as soon as his lectures were finished. But he met a wealthy Bostonian, Abbott Lawrence, and they talked together about the Swiss and the German universities where Agassiz had studied natural science. American boys could find no such courses in their own country. Mr. Lawrence decided to give fifty thousand dollars to start the Lawrence Scientific School at Harvard University.

As soon as he knew that the Scientific School was really going to open, Mr. Lawrence wrote to Agassiz asking him to become Professor of Zoology and Geology. Although he did not realize it, Agassiz had fallen in love with America. He wanted to study the whole great continent with its mountains, its forests, its lakes and great rivers. Here was his chance and he agreed to become a Harvard professor at last during the next three years.

Agassiz wrote to Cecile and the children. How would they like to come to America? It was a wonderful place. Surely Cecile's cough was better, but a sea voyage might do her a world of good. Letters sent across the ocean by sailing ship, then carried inland by horse-drawn coach, took a long time on their journey. Months went by before answers to Agassiz's questions could reach the United States from northern Germany.

Agassiz wanted to explore the Rocky Mountains, but he never could get used to the size of the United States compared with his native Switzerland. He thought he might get to the Rockies in a few days before the Harvard term began. But there was no railroad to take him across the great plains and he was finally convinced that it would take not days but months to cross the continent to the Pacific coast. He settled for a trip to the White Mountains in New Hampshire.

"Why do you call this the 'New World'?" Agassiz exclaimed as he examined the many "striated" glacial rocks on the slopes of Mount Washington. "These mountains are volcanic," he told the friends who went with him. "They rose many millions of years ago and, after that, great ice floes smoothed and ground them down." Later a mountain in New Hampshire was named Mount Agassiz, and on the Moosilauke River near Woodstock is Agassiz Basin, full of ice-worn boulders and deep potholes.

Years went by before Agassiz saw the Rockies. Then he pointed out that they were "new" in the long story of the earth. They were sharp-edged and not ice-worn. And in the Rockies a much higher Mount Agassiz reminds people of the Swiss naturalist who opened the eyes of Americans to the wonders of their own country.

Louis Agassiz was the first foreign-born and foreign-educated professor to teach at Harvard. He was something new at that old New England college, with his French-style broad-brimmed hat and his big cigar. As he walked across Harvard Yard, he had such a friendly smile for everyone that everybody liked him.

Agassiz's house in Cambridge was different from other professors' houses. In the cellar he kept a tame bear. There were turtles in the bathtub, turtles under the stairs — turtles everywhere. In the back yard Agassiz had a small alligator in a tank, a hutch full of rabbits, a family of opossums in a cage and an eagle chained to a perch. The eagle got away one day and in spite of clipped wings it managed to cross neighbors' gardens for several blocks. Some of Agassiz's students set out after it. They finally cornered it, but it tore at them with its beak and talons before they could carry it back to its perch.

Many refugees came to America from Switzerland at about this time. Switzerland was going through a struggle for the independence of some of the cantons, and if the refugees were scientists they came to Agassiz. He made everyone welcome and gave money to all who needed it until sometimes he had none left for himself. He tried hard to find places where foreign scientists could teach but some of them had first to learn English and all this took time. Agassiz sometimes had as many as twenty-two guests living at his house. When there were not beds enough for them they just slept on the floor.

Agassiz gave wonderful open-house parties on Sunday nights. Students were welcome as well as other Harvard professors and visiting foreign scientists. It might have been hard to find food enough for all these guests except that people were always sending specimens to Agassiz and some of these specimens were good to eat. Turtles not needed for study made fine soup. Once a caribou arrived from Maine "frozen entire," as Agassiz said. Frozen food is common enough now, but in 1848 Agassiz was probably the only person to cook frozen caribou.

Agassiz kept a barrel of good German beer in his cellar for his guests. One night the more or less tame bear got loose and helped himself to the beer. Then he came up the stairs to see what was going on. He found a big table with wonderful food on it all smoking hot. Around the table sat Agassiz's friends at one of their Sunday night supper parties. The bear paid no attention to the people but climbed up on the table and began eating the food. The guests did not stop to find out if the bear was really tame or not. They ran.

During the first summer vacation, Agassiz took an assistant and eleven Harvard students on a scientific expedition to the Great Lakes. This was something he had always wanted to do ever since he was a student himself and he was as excited as though he were still a boy.

Agassiz brought along a piece of oilcloth painted black

and fastened to a roller like a window shade. This was his portable blackboard. When the train got to Albany, where they spent the first night, Agassiz told his students that he would lecture on the country they had just passed through. He began by asking the boys what they had observed from the windows of the train. To Agassiz's amazement, his students had noticed little or nothing. It was summer. Air conditioning was still undreamed of, and the boys had been hot and covered with dust. Black smoke poured out of the engine as it puffed along and some of the students had gotten cinders in their eyes. Nobody had noticed that "the exposed rocks were all erratic" and had been brought from some other place.

But by the time the students reached the Great Lakes they had begun to use their eyes regardless of heat and cinders. They noticed that different kinds of trees grew in different kinds of soil. The birds they saw were not the same as those at home. Every evening Agassiz lectured and questioned his students, teaching them to use ears and eyes and to figure out answers for themselves when something puzzled them. Most of the students were city boys and it was almost as if they had been blind and deaf. Now they learned to see and hear.

On Lake Superior, Agassiz encountered his first American Indians. Here were "aborigines," people who had lived in America before the first European settlers

came, and Agassiz had always wanted to study such people. He had very little trouble in talking to them because
some of them had come down the Lake from Canada
and spoke French. He hired birchbark canoes and Indian guides to paddle them. There were buffalo robes
for covering at night and Agassiz remembered the

North American buffalo which he had admired in the museum at Stuttgart in far-away Germany. He still wanted to see a living buffalo.

Agassiz's enthusiasm made it fun for his students to be with him. The whole Great Lakes expedition was like a vacation camping trip. But at the same time, Agassiz expected his students to work hard. In spite of rain, he and the Indians went out to catch fish. The students, who had been taught to go in when it rained, felt quite ashamed of themselves. They got to work regardless of the weather collecting plants, fresh-water shells, minerals or whatever had been assigned to them. One of them made careful drawings of rock formations. At night Agassiz lectured and questioned the students, who also asked questions. There was time to sing songs around the campfire and to tell stories. But more and more often, Agassiz's students found themselves talking like scientists, interested most of all in the wilderness they were exploring.

Everyone made a collection. Professor Agassiz's own specimens filled four barrels and twelve big boxes. As usual, there was difficulty in persuading the baggage men on trains to be careful of the precious freight. But Agassiz's collection arrived safely in Cambridge and now the trouble was to find a place to put it. There was no museum in Cambridge as there had been in the little city of Neuchâtel. The Lawrence Scientific School was new and no one had thought very much about the specimens that students would want to study. Agassiz began to talk to friends about building a museum.

Harvard gave Agassiz a small wooden building for his collections and it was soon full to overflowing. Agassiz worried for fear the wooden building would catch fire. Every time he heard the clang of fire bells and saw the big gray fire horses galloping down the street pulling the steam water-pumper, he dashed out of his house. He would look anxiously in the direction of his little wooden laboratory and museum — sure that he would see smoke rising.

"We must build a brick museum and make it as fire-proof as possible," Agassiz told everyone. And people who knew Agassiz best were sure that he would get his building. When he set his heart on something important he never stopped working for it until he had reached his goal.

Swiss Children in America

WHEN Agassiz returned to Cambridge after his summer on the Great Lakes, many letters from Germany and Switzerland were waiting for him. There were portraits of the children which Cecile had drawn for him in pencil. Agassiz searched eagerly for a letter which might say that his family would soon come to the United States. But Cecile had grown weaker instead of stronger. There were sad letters telling him that she had died.

The two little girls, Ida and Pauline, had gone to live with their grandmother in Switzerland, and Agassiz wrote to his mother begging her to send all the children to America. But she decided that the girls were too young to go and Alex, thirteen years old, set out alone. The sailing vessel in which he crossed the Atlantic was forty-five days at sea before it reached New York. There on the dock his father was waiting for him.

Alex spoke not a word of English, and as soon as he and his father arrived in Cambridge his father took him to a party. Poor Alex was rather a shy boy and he was quite scared when he walked into a room full of older people all speaking a strange language. He remembered his proper German manners which his mother had taught him. So he clicked his heels together and bowed from the waist when introduced to people. And then he noticed that nobody else did that! He could feel his face growing hot with embarrassment. He looked across the room and saw a young lady smiling at him in an especially friendly way. She looked as though she understood just how he felt. She was Miss Elizabeth Cary. When Alex talked with her, he forgot to be shy.

The next weekend, Alex and his father went to Nahant to visit Miss Cary and her family. Nahant was a hard name to pronounce for a boy who spoke only French and German. Alex found that it was a rocky headland near Boston with a little fishing village and also houses where people went for the summer. There were cliffs to climb and small sandy beaches fine for swimming — if only the water had not been so cold. Here the Carys had a stone house on a hill high above the sea. It was filled with people — Miss Cary's father and mother, her brothers and sisters, and all their children. Many of the boys and girls were Alex's age but none of them spoke French or German. They were wonderfully friendly, however, and Miss Cary, who spoke French, helped them to get acquainted. Alex solved the language problem. He could talk in Latin and he found that the American boys could talk Latin too and so could some of the girls. Now they all began to have a good time.

Alexander Agassiz loved natural history just as much as his father did. When he was only nine his father taught him to dissect and mount fish and to skin and mount small animals. Alex was a very gentle boy — too gentle and shy, his father sometimes thought. But if anyone meddled with his collections he flew into a rage. It made no difference if it was a bigger boy who teased him — that boy would be wise to run.

In Cambridge, Alex went to high school, where he learned English very quickly. Harvard had a long winter vacation and Agassiz went to Charleston, South Carolina, where he gave lectures in anatomy at the Charleston Medical College. He took Alex along. Alex was his father's assistant and he worked hard, but he also had a good time.

Great white houses with high pillared porches had been built just outside Charleston. They were on rivers and were surrounded by rice fields where hundreds of Negro slaves worked all day. The owners of the rice plantations had become rich and some of them had taken up natural science as a hobby. Agassiz was soon acquainted with them all and was invited to visit them at the mansion houses. There were thoroughbred saddle horses for Alex to ride. He learned to dance the Virginia reel — the girls his age always seemed to be visiting and giving parties for each other all up and down the rivers at the big houses.

One of the plantation owners let the water out of his rice fields so that Agassiz could see what kind of fresh-

water creatures lived in the South Carolina mud. Alex
was proud to be allowed to study and describe many an
ugly-looking worm. The girls were a little annoyed with
him when he forgot all about them while working with
worms.

The house in Cambridge with all its strange animals
pleased Alex too, but he was lonely for his sisters. Perhaps he did not know that his father kept writing to the
grandmother in Switzerland, asking her to let Ida and
Pauline come to America. But Agassiz's mother had very
strict ideas. She said always that a house full of scientists
and strange animals was no place for little girls.

In April, 1850, Louis Agassiz married Miss Elizabeth
Cary of Boston. Now all those boys and girls Alex had
met at Nahant were his cousins. Now the two Swiss
girls could come to America and they very soon arrived.
Ida would be thirteen in August and Pauline was nine.
They traveled all alone to New York and they were sad
to leave their grandmother. Maybe they had read some
fairy stories about mean stepmothers, too, and they had
no idea what their own stepmother would be like.

Alex was now fifteen. He was sent to the railroad station in Boston, just a few miles away, to bring the girls
out to their new home in Cambridge. When the train
came in, he thought it would be fun to see if his sisters
recognized him before he spoke to them. Ida and Pauline
had been carefully taught to pay no attention to strange

boys, and when they got off the train they never so much as glanced at him. Alex followed to see what they would do. They would be scared, he thought, when they saw all the horses and carriages out on the street and heard the rumble of wheels on the cobblestones as drays went by loaded with hides or grain. Then he would come forward and rescue them.

But Ida and Pauline were not scared. They looked for an omnibus marked Cambridge, found it and got inside. Off went the bus, leaving Alex behind. The girls, who spoke no English, got off at Harvard Square, having learned how the name sounded, whether they could pronounce it or not. Someone must have drawn them a little map — just in case they needed it — for they found Oxford Street. Then down Oxford Street they came without any help at all.

Alex arrived at their father's house just behind the girls. He was much out of breath and very red in the face. He knew he deserved a scolding. But the girls were made to feel that they had proved themselves wonderful travelers. Their stepmother talked to them in French but seemed anxious about it as if she feared she couldn't say all she wanted to. Ida and Pauline found themselves trying to help her out and they forgot to be afraid of her. They could see that she was really happy because they had come. Before long the girls loved her dearly. And Alex was already calling her "Ma."

The house on Oxford Street was not large enough,
now that Agassiz had his family with him. He built a
new house at the corner of Quincy Street and Broadway,
right opposite Harvard Yard. There were plenty of rooms

for everybody and Agassiz had the kind of laboratory he had always dreamed of. When he was a boy he longed to own a microscope. Now he had the best that could be made and it was mounted on a pedestal set in a rock ledge so that nothing could jar it.

When people build exactly the kind of house they want, it is apt to cost a good deal. Agassiz still hated to keep accounts, so it was Mrs. Agassiz who talked things over with the children. "If we started a school for girls, we could earn some money," she suggested. Alex promised to be a teacher in the school and so did Ida. But Pauline was too young — she would have to be a pupil.

Now they were all a little worried lest Father might not like the idea of having a lot of schoolgirls all over his house every weekday. But Louis Agassiz was one of the few people, in those days, who thought that girls ought to be allowed to study the same things that boys did. He said he would love to teach natural science in the school.

There was not even a high school for girls in Boston or Cambridge at this time, so a great many pupils wanted to come to Mrs. Agassiz's school. They had to hire a bus, drawn by two horses, which stopped at certain street corners in Boston to pick up the girls. Then it rumbled along over the Charles River and down a dusty country road to Cambridge, where it stopped on Quincy Street at Mrs. Agassiz's door. Some of the girls rode their own horses to school! A boy from the livery stable, where horses and carriages could be hired, would come to the Agassiz house in the morning. He would untie the saddle horses from the hitching posts and would take them to the stable, then bring them back when school was over.

Agassiz kept his promise, and his lessons in natural history were the most popular of all the courses at the school. To be sure, he brought a nice harmless little snake in his pocket one morning. When he took it out and held it gently while it wriggled in his hands some of the girls thought they ought to scream. He laughed at them and told them not to be silly. Then he began to tell them interesting things about snakes and before long most of them forgot about being afraid.

In summer, the whole Agassiz family usually went to Nahant. Mrs. Agassiz's father bought her a small white house in the village and had it moved on rollers up to the top of the cliff near his own stone house. It was so small they called it the "Butter Box." But they added a wing on one side for the children with extra rooms for some of their cousins and their friends. Mrs. Agassiz had grown up with four sisters and two brothers of her own and she loved a big family. On the other side of the house they built a laboratory for Agassiz.

Agassiz was always fond of Nahant — almost an island, joined to the mainland only by a sandy strip, with waves breaking over the road in stormy weather. Agassiz could look out of his window and see nothing

but ocean with here and there a white sail. He soon made friends with all the fishermen down in the village and if they found a strange-looking fish in their nets they would bring it to him. Sometimes they had to row a dory a long distance after the day's work was done but Agassiz always made them welcome. He would invite them into his laboratory and exclaim over the fish they had brought. They went away feeling proud because they were important to the work of a scientist.

Agassiz himself went fishing at Nahant. He had become fascinated by jellyfish and his whole family loved to go jellyfishing with him. August was the best time. About eleven in the morning was soon enough if the tide was right — it should be rising. They kept a dory on the little beach beyond the cliffs in front of the house. And down the cliff path they went, carrying pails, nets and some glass bowls.

Alex usually took the oars. He rowed slowly along shore toward a nearby ledge, everyone watching for a blue or a pale lavender jelly-like blob in the water. How excited they got when they saw one that looked a little different from all the others! "Stop!" Pauline would cry out to Alex. But you can't stop a boat instantly. "Back a little," Pauline would have to say. "Now left — no, not so far." The oarsman had the hardest job.

The others would have nets out by now. If the jellyfish looked very small and delicate, Ida would try to

catch it in a glass bowl while her father kept a net under it so it could not get away. They had to be careful to put big jellyfish in jars by themselves or they would eat little ones. Mrs. Agassiz saw how much fun the children had, not only catching jellyfish but learning about them. She wrote a book about sea creatures for her children, her nieces and nephews and their friends, and Alex drew the pictures for it.

12

The Big Museum

SUMMERS AT NAHANT always ended too soon. But Agassiz loved to teach the boys who came to him at the Lawrence Scientific School. They reminded him of the days when he was an eager young student at Heidelberg and Munich, wanting so much to learn about the world of nature. When students came who had hardly any money, he always tried to help them out. He knew just how it felt to be hungry and to have no new clothes to wear. His own salary was never very large but he paid many a boy as an "assistant" so that the boy could stay in school. However, he was often disappointed because American boys were not willing to work as hard as German students.

There were no entrance examinations for the Lawrence Scientific School in Agassiz's time. A boy came to Cambridge, hunted up the professor whose classes he wanted to attend, and was asked some questions. Then the professor told him whether or not he could stay. Nathaniel Shaler from Kentucky told how it was when he went to see Agassiz. Shaler had read an article on turtles which Agassiz had written. This was what gave him the idea that he wanted to be a naturalist, and when Agassiz questioned him about the article he remembered what he had read. The article had contained references to other articles and some books. Shaler had looked those up and read them. He knew enough Latin so that he could understand scientific terms and he could read both French and German. This pleased Agassiz because many books on natural science were written in either French or German.

A student should be strong and healthy and today a boy's athletic record is important. In Agassiz's day there were no football teams. When Agassiz was a student the sport was fencing, so he asked young Shaler if he could fence. Shaler said he could. He had been brought up at a military post and had taken fencing lessons from a French fencing faster. Agassiz told him to get his foils and they had a bout.

Agassiz fenced in the German style, Shaler said afterwards. Shaler felt that he himself won the bout — he did not know that Agassiz had never had any fencing lessons. But Agassiz was pleased and surprised to find an American boy who could fence so well. He told Shaler to come to the laboratory next day.

Shaler's testing was not really over. He went to the wooden building where Agassiz's collections were kept and climbed to the second floor. A room about thirty feet long and half as wide was full of students all working in mysterious ways on specimens of various kinds. Shaler was told to sit down at a small pine table. A tin

pan was put in front of him and in it was a fish which
had been preserved in alcohol. Shaler was told not to
speak to anyone and not to look at any books. He was
just to study the fish. He might pick it up and look it
over but he must not injure the specimen. It smelled
horribly of stale alcohol but he must not let it get dry.

Shaler sat and stared at the fish. He had no idea how
to begin studying it but he got out a notebook and wrote
down a few things he noticed. He counted its fins. It had
a forked tail and he wrote that down. Finally he counted
the scales and put down the number. After about an
hour he felt he knew all there was to know about that
ugly little fish. Agassiz was in the room all this time. He
seemed to be busy first with one student and then with
another. Two hours went by and still Agassiz paid no
attention to the new pupil.

"When you have done the work I will question you,"
Agassiz had said. But the whole day went by. Then a
week passed. Now Shaler realized that here was a new
kind of test. He tore up his first notes and went to work
much more carefully. Starting at the nose of his fish, he
examined every inch of it all the way to the tail. He discovered about a hundred times more facts about that
fish than he supposed anyone could know. The scales
were an odd shape, he found. And they changed in size,
being rather large near the fish's head and small at its
tail. All he got from Agassiz was a cheerful "Good morn-

ing" each day. But at last, after a second week, Agassiz came and sat on the corner of Shaler's table. "Well?" he said.

Shaler rather proudly told all he knew about the little fish. "That's not right," said Agassiz when Shaler had finished. Then he went away leaving Shaler to find out for himself exactly what was not right and why.

Shaler almost gave up natural science then and there. But he realized he was still being tested. He began all over again and found his own mistakes. After another week of working about ten hours a day he surprised himself, he said. And Agassiz was pleased.

Next Shaler was given what looked like at least half a peck of fish bones. He was told that they belonged to various different kinds of fish and he was to sort them out. He put a head here, a tail there, and tried to figure out which ribs belonged to which fish. It was the hardest puzzle he had ever tackled but Shaler found that he was having fun. Now and then Agassiz looked over his shoulder. He would point out something and usually he said "That's not right." But even this much was a help. Shaler finally got his fish bones properly sorted into separate fish.

He next worked on about twenty "side-swimmers" preserved in alcohol. Finally he graduated to animals, learning to compare one kind with another all the way along. It gave him "a sense of power," he said. Now he knew he could go out into a wilderness with notebook and pencil and be able to classify almost anything he saw.

At last Shaler was allowed to read books. But Agassiz always warned his students that the books might not be right. They must learn to observe directly from nature and they must always think for themselves. Shaler was now allowed to talk with the other students too and they had exciting discussions about their work.

Louis Agassiz had always studied very hard just for the pleasure of finding out the things he wanted to know. He regarded college degrees as more or less of a mere ornament. To think of the degree of Bachelor of Science from the Lawrence Scientific School as the *only* reason for going there was like imagining that a man's hat was more important than his head. But American students had a practical streak. They wanted to earn their living as natural scientists and a degree was the best way of telling people that they knew their subject. There was no such thing as completing certain courses with Agassiz and then getting a degree, however. Students had to tell him they wanted to take their examinations and he usually said they hadn't learned half enough.

Nathaniel Shaler told how he got his own B.S. degree. After he had worked with Agassiz four years, he told his professor that he was ready for examinations. "Nonsense," said Agassiz. "What makes you think so?"

In all the four years, Shaler had been given no examinations at all. But Agassiz constantly questioned him during laboratory hours. Shaler had self-confidence, however, and he finally persuaded Agassiz to let him have his examinations. Seven professors and the President of Harvard gathered early one morning and Shaler, all alone, was told to sit in a chair on a platform. There was a blackboard behind him and when he was not at the blackboard he was sitting in the chair for the next five hours, with time out for lunch. Agassiz began the questions.

Now Shaler discovered that Agassiz was really proud of him and wanted him to make a good impression. The questions were the ones Shaler could answer best. Then Agassiz began a sort of debate so that Shaler could show that he had done original work. "My Master put me at my ease," Shaler said. He found himself talking to the seven professors and the President as easily as though they had been fellow students.

Agassiz's questions took two hours. Then the other professors began. Shaler was asked about botany, zoology and mineralogy. He had dreaded questions by the teacher of mathematics because that was his weak subject. But he was asked about "mountain building" and he had just read up on mountains. Nathaniel Shaler received his degree with highest honors.

Agassiz was one of the most remarkable teachers at

Harvard University. But he had not given up his boy-
hood ambition to be the head of a great museum. In
1858, the ambition could have been realized — Agassiz
was asked to be the head of the Jardin des Plantes in
Paris. Here was the very thing which people had laughed
at him for wanting when he was a boy. But he refused
the offer!

Once Agassiz had thought of the Jardin des Plantes
as the greatest museum in the world. But he had been a
boy from the small country of Switzerland then, and
now he lived in the United States. His ideas had grown
as big as the United States — compared to Switzerland.
Agassiz now thought of the Jardin des Plantes as much
too small and he wanted to build a really big museum
and direct it himself. The best place for it would not be
Paris, France, but Cambridge, Massachusetts, he thought.

If Agassiz had still been living in Europe, he would
have looked around for a king or a prince rich enough to
build him a huge museum. In America, the thing to do
was to look for a businessman. Francis Calley Gray,
whose fortune came from shoe factories in Lynn, Massachusetts, was just the man. Now came the question of
what to name the museum. Everybody thought it ought
to be the Agassiz. Louis Agassiz himself said that natural
science was more important than any one man. Mr. Gray
agreed, so the name was neither the Gray nor the Agassiz, but the Museum of Comparative Zoology.

The great brick buildings on Oxford Street are called exactly that. But hardly anyone knows this name. People come by busloads to see the "glass flowers," which were made by a German family for students of botany. Visitors who know about Agassiz want to see some of the fossil fish he discovered and named. The museum has passed its hundredth birthday, but ever since it was first built people have called it the Agassiz. Science is more important than one man: that is true. But Louis Agassiz taught so many people to appreciate natural science that they could not help giving his museum his name.

13

Off to Brazil

AS SOON AS the museum building was begun in 1859, Agassiz, his wife and his daughter Pauline set out for Europe. Agassiz had come to the United States as a visitor and he had stayed almost thirteen years. Now he felt like a visitor in Switzerland but he still loved the Alps. The mountain air made him feel like a boy again. His father had died, but he visited his mother, who was living with one of his sisters on the Lake of Neuchâtel. Everyone was proud of Louis because he had traveled so far and had become such a famous man. It was Augustus who was especially interested in the new museum.

Agassiz met fellow scientists too, and everywhere he went he asked about collections that might be for sale. Most tourists love to go shopping in Europe. But Agassiz was a different sort of traveler. Instead of buying Swiss watches and wood carvings or Paris clothes, he shopped for fossil fish and shells for his new museum. American students of natural history used to go to Europe to study. "When my Museum of Comparative Zoology is complete," Agassiz declared, "European scholars will have to come to America."

After Agassiz and his family got back to America, crates and boxes began to arrive. It was like Christmas

every day for Agassiz. As he unpacked the collections he had bought he would call out to his students in the laboratory to come and see what he had for them. It was important, Agassiz thought, for a student to be able to handle specimens — to get the weight and the feel of fossils in his hand, for example. So he tried to have not one but many examples of different things. Some fossils are very delicate and he felt badly if a student dropped and broke one. But accidents will happen.

"How much did you pay for these?" one boy asked, unwrapping some shells.

"About ten cents apiece," said Agassiz. "But they are scarce. Someday they will be worth three hundred dollars at least."

After Agassiz had sold his own first collection to the Museum of Neuchâtel, he had started collecting all over again. At the time the new museum was being built, Agassiz had been working on his second collection for twenty-seven years and it was enormous. Once more a subscription was raised, many different people giving money, and Agassiz's new collection was bought for fifty thousand dollars.

An important part of Agassiz's teaching was his way of comparing one thing with another. He had the skeleton of a heavy work horse, for example, handsomely mounted. It was easy to see what strong but rather short leg bones it had. Now Agassiz wanted the skeleton of a race horse to put beside it. Leg bones of a race horse would be long and slender. Agassiz asked his pupil Nathaniel Shaler if he could get the skeleton of a race horse because Shaler, being from Kentucky, knew people who raised horses. But Shaler did not know of anyone who would give Agassiz the skeleton of a thoroughbred.

And then one night there was the clang of fire bells and a red glow in the sky. Word spread that the fire was at a race track on the outskirts of Cambridge, and college students rushed to see the blaze. Shaler was just coming back from the fire when he met Agassiz going out to see it. "What a wonderful chance!" Agassiz exclaimed. "I shall get my race horse skeleton."

Shaler was horrified. People out at the race track were already angry because they thought someone had set the fire on purpose, and they were unhappy because many fine horses had been killed. If a stranger came along asking for horse skeletons, people would be both angry and suspicious. He begged Agassiz to stay away, and when Agassiz would not, Shaler went along to protect him.

But young Shaler did not entirely understand Agassiz. The first thing Agassiz did when he got to the race track was to help the horses that could be saved. He knew of remedies for burns and he set stable hands to work. Nobody asked who he was or thought him queer because he had a foreign accent. "It was plain that he loved horses and knew a great deal about them," Shaler said.

When everything had been done that could be done to save the horses that were still alive, Agassiz brought up the matter of his museum. And now everybody wanted to help him in return. It was heartbreaking to have the horses die but it would be some comfort if the bones of one of them could be used to teach people. Agassiz could have his choice.

Agassiz was very happy labeling and listing his specimens. He planned beautiful rooms where specimens could be arranged for people to see. He told artists how he wanted pictures painted so that people who happened to come into the museum just to look around could easily learn about the world they lived in. There were to be pictures showing the oldest of the sea creatures, worms and water plants. Then there would be the fish and reptiles.

But before all this could be done, the Civil War broke out. It seemed to Agassiz as if clouds had rolled over the sun.

Some said that Agassiz sympathized with the South. This was not true. He believed that slavery was wrong but he hoped it could be stopped without a war. There were both Southern and Northern boys in his classes and he loved them all. Agassiz knew that both sides were going to lose some of their finest young men and he thought especially of great discoveries in natural science that would be long in coming because the boys who might have made them would not live to do their work in the world. Many of Agassiz's students volunteered on both sides, and they never quite understood why Agassiz was so sad.

There was one thing he was glad to hear about. One of his students in the Northern army collected shells on a beach in South Carolina. Men in the Southern army let him come through their lines to get specimens.

During the Civil War, work at the museum was almost at a standstill. Agassiz hardly knew what to do. And then one more of his dreams came true. Ever since he had worked on the book about Brazilian fishes at the University of Munich he had wanted to go to Brazil. And now Nathaniel Thayer, a wealthy Bostonian, offered to give all the money needed for an expedition to Brazil for Agassiz.

As soon as word got around that Agassiz was going to Brazil, boys and young men who could not get into the army begged to go with Agassiz. Ernest Longfellow, son of Henry Wadsworth Longfellow, was "wild to go," he said. But his father said he was too young. William James, later famous as a psychologist and philosopher, won his parents' consent. So did Renwick Thayer, son of the man who gave the money for the expedition. In all, there were six assistants, five students and Mrs. Agassiz, in the party.

The Pacific Mail Steamship Company had ships going

to California by way of Cape Horn. Ships had been full of passengers when the gold rush was going on, but that was over now, it was wartime, and in April, 1865, the steamship *Colorado* was setting out from New York almost empty of passengers. The president of the steamship company gave Agassiz free passage for himself and his whole party. Agassiz was much pleased because he wanted to make Mr. Thayer's gift last as long as possible.

People loved Agassiz and were always giving him presents. His cabin on board ship looked like a huge Christmas stocking full of gifts, one of his friends said. There were oranges, apples, chocolate drops, books and newspapers. There were all sorts of scientific instruments, some of them gifts, some of them bought by Agassiz. He paced the deck in great anxiety just before the ship sailed because a new barometer he had ordered had not come. Agassiz's cousin who sold watches had found a Swiss artisan in New York to make this fine instrument. And at last here came a little wizened man, just in time. He had been making some last-minute adjustments and he didn't seem to realize that the ship would have sailed without the barometer.

Agassiz had been up all night making sure that everything was ready for the expedition. In the ship's hold were barrels for the specimens he intended to send back to the museum from Brazil. They were as yet just a collection of staves and heads because they would take up less room that way. But Agassiz remembered exactly how the barrel-maker back in Switzerland had gone to work. He would teach one of his students to be a cooper. There was alcohol for preserving fish and there were nets and lines for catching them. Guns had been brought along to shoot everything from parakeets to tigers. (Mrs. Agassiz would be pleased when members of the party missed while trying to shoot parakeets.)

"You must take a rest as soon as the ship sails," one of Agassiz's friends said.

"Nonsense," said Agassiz. "As soon as we leave New York harbor, I shall start taking the temperature of the water and recording it."

Agassiz wanted to know exactly where the cold waters of the Atlantic gave place to the warm waters of the Gulf Stream. Benjamin Franklin had been the first to measure the temperature of the Gulf Stream, Agassiz said. Now the American Coast Survey would be the first to chart its course and Agassiz had promised to help in this project.

The water began to be warm off Cape Hatteras. At that point the Gulf Stream was sixty miles wide. The warmest temperature Agassiz listed was 74 degrees.

Sailors helped Agassiz to collect the special kind of seaweed that floats in the Gulf Stream. The captain of

the ship had a tank set up on deck where everything
could be kept alive in sea water. And every evening Agassiz gave a lecture to his students about all the things they
had seen and all they caught and collected during the

day. The sailors were so interested that if they were off
duty, they came to the lectures too.

Agassiz had brought along his portable blackboard —
the one with black oilcloth on a roller like a window
shade. On board ship he took two leaves out of the big
table where passengers ate their meals and set those up —
covered with black oilcloth. The pictures of sea creatures
which Agassiz drew in chalk pleased everyone. He did
them very quickly but he knew so well just how they
should go that he never had to change a line. His sketches
were as beautiful as the best Japanese pen-and-ink drawings, people said. And when Agassiz was through telling
about a sketch he had made and erased it, people were
sorry to see it go.

Most of the sea animals found among the gulfweed
had never before been described. Many would now have
the name *Agassii* after them in museums. Agassiz warned
his students that they must be very careful about putting labels on the specimens they collected. Each label
must tell where the specimen was found and the date
when found. Labels must be fastened tightly so they
would still be on the specimen when it got back to Cambridge. "And when we get to Brazil," Agassiz said, "we
must try never to mix the fishes of different rivers, even
though the rivers flow into each other."

But Brazil seemed a long way off and the *Colorado*
was at sea for twenty days before Agassiz and his party

saw pointed mountain peaks. The ship entered a passage between two high cliffs, rising like castle towers guarding a gate. They entered a bay that was more than twenty miles wide so that it looked almost like a lake. It was the harbor of Rio de Janeiro.

14

U*p the Amazon*

IN 1865 Brazil was ruled by an emperor, Dom Pedro II. As soon as the *Colorado* came to anchor at the port of Rio de Janeiro, Agassiz went ashore to meet the Emperor at his palace. Foreigners were not particularly welcome in Brazil at that time. Agassiz wanted to go up the Amazon and the Amazon was closed to everyone except Brazilians.

But Louis Agassiz was not at all worried. He always made friends wherever he went and it turned out that the Emperor had been to school in Switzerland. Dom Pedro was also much interested in natural history and that was all that Agassiz needed. He and the Emperor talked half the afternoon and Agassiz promised to bring a microscope next time he came to the palace. They would look at some of the specimens caught on the voyage and Agassiz would tell the Emperor all about them.

As for going up the Amazon — the Emperor not only gave his consent but arranged for Agassiz to have the use of a small steam yacht. A Brazilian army officer, Major Coutinho, would go along as guide. All the arrangements would take time, however, so the Emperor invited Professor and Mrs. Agassiz to take a ride on the new railroad which was only partly finished.

An open car with seats in it was fastened in front of the engine and off into the Brazilian jungle they went. This was Agassiz's first glimpse of a South American forest. Huge trees were laced together with vines. Orchids, large and small, grew from the trunks of the trees and from the branches. There were no paths in the forest and the railroad train seemed to run between green walls. Agassiz looked hopefully for snakes among the vines on all the tree trunks. This was where the Brazilian anaconda, one of the world's largest snakes, liked best to live.

One of Agassiz's Brazilian friends told him that the anaconda grew to be forty feet long and that it could crush an animal the size of a calf within its coils — then open its jaws and swallow the calf whole. Of course Agassiz wanted a forty-foot anaconda for his museum. But his Brazilian friends were telling tall tales. The late Dr. Raymond L. Ditmars, famous Curator of Mammals and Reptiles at the New York Zoological Park, was to list the South American anaconda as the world's third largest snake, those in Burma coming first. Dr. Ditmars said he never knew of one that actually measured much over twenty-two feet. So Agassiz need not have been so disappointed when he never got exactly the anaconda he was looking for.

This early Brazilian railroad soon left the low-lying country where the big trees grew. It climbed steeply into the mountains to reach the hill country and the coffee plantations. The railroad was being built to carry the coffee harvest to the seacoast and soon there would be no more long processions of mules winding through the mountain passes with huge bags of coffee on their backs. But there was no earth-moving machinery at this time. Three hundred men, working in shifts night and day for seven years, had not yet been able to finish the railroad. Temporary tracks had been laid part of the way with curves so sharp that the car in front of the engine, where Agassiz rode, seemed about to bump into the rear of the train. People in the open railroad car could look down over a cliff to a rushing stream thousands of feet below. Soon the train crossed the stream on a shaky wooden bridge.

"Weren't you afraid?" people asked Agassiz when he got back to Rio.

"I never saw more interesting volcanic formations than those cliffs," said Agassiz. "I must have forgotten to be afraid. By the way, can you tell me where I can get an anaconda?"

On the 27th of May, the night before Agassiz's birthday, a dinner was given for him by the Swiss people living in Rio de Janeiro. The hall was decorated with flags of all the different cantons while two big Swiss national flags covered the ceiling. Behind Agassiz's chair was the flag of the United States, because in 1863 Agassiz had become a United States citizen. His Swiss friends in Rio knew that he was proud of his new country and that his country was proud of him.

It was a fine party. There were songs and speeches of course. A poem written about Agassiz by Longfellow had been translated into French and this was read. The Emperor himself came to do honor to Agassiz, and Agassiz enjoyed every minute. But he was beginning to be impatient to be off up the Amazon and he had discovered that there was a favorite word in Brazil. "Tomorrow," everyone said. Nothing ever got done today. It was always "tomorrow."

There was time for Professor and Mrs. Agassiz to have an audience with the Empress of Brazil. They passed between palace guards, they were led down long corridors and through many rooms. Finally they reached a parlor with heavy mahogany furniture and velvet curtains. The Emperor came in and talked to Agassiz. Was he getting plenty of fish?

Agassiz said yes but politely suggested that he would like to get on with his expedition.

At last in came the Empress Theresa Maria. She was "a fat little lady, not at all pretty," Mrs. Agassiz said. But she had a nice, motherly expression and she asked after the Agassiz children.

There was time in Rio to attend the opening of Chambers, as the Brazilian legislature was called. Agassiz and his wife sat in good seats where they could see everything. The Emperor marched in wearing a tight-fitting suit of white satin, white shoes with rosettes on them and a green velvet cape with a long train. Page boys carried his train and they were dressed in satin too. The Emperor wore a gold crown on his head and carried a scepter in his hand just like a king in a fairy tale. And the Empress had a huge emerald in her crown that seemed to glow with a light of its own.

When the ceremonies were over, the Emperor drove off in a great glass coach with a big gold crown on top of it. The Empress had a coach of her own, drawn by eight white horses.

At last it was time to set out for the Amazon. Rio is south of the Amazon, so Agassiz and his expedition went aboard a dirty, crowded little coastwise steamer, headed north. It took them seventeen days, with various stopovers at small ports, to reach Para, an important town in the rubber trade. Here yellow patches stained the blue water of the South Atlantic and told of the muddy Amazon — still far away.

At Para, Louis Agassiz had his first sight of a kind of boat he would come to know very well. It was a canoe called a *montaria*. At the stern was a cubbyhole of a cabin with a thatched roof. The wooden boat was long, narrow and rather flat so it could go in shallow water. Fishermen, with wife and children, lived aboard these boats. They slept in woven grass hammocks at night and the women did all the family cooking over a pan of glowing charcoal. Meals were simple. There was always fish, there was tapioca and coffee, but that was all. Many canoes with families living in them clustered around Para. They made a water-borne city close to the city on land.

Agassiz hired some men to take him fishing in some of the clear streams that ran into the bay at Para. The men carried no fishpoles nor any hook and line. They had just one good-sized net and this they slung across a stream. Then they went upstream and waded in. Now they shouted and splashed and tossed stones like boys playing in a brook. All the time they kept moving down stream and when they got to their net it was full of fish! Agassiz had never seen so many fish caught so easily before.

Now it was the turn of the fishermen to be surprised. The "wise man," as they called Agassiz, did not seem to want the fish that were good to eat. The ones the people would have thrown away were the ones he wanted most to keep. These were the strange ones, to be sure, and Agassiz was as excited as a boy with his first trout when he found a fish with four eyes! Actually, each eye was divided into two halves. The lower half could see under water and the upper half could see in the air. These fish live in shallows and leap along rather like frogs. But Agassiz had to study his new specimen carefully before he found out all this about his four-eyed fish. In waters near Para, he found fifty fish that had never before been described.

The small steamer which the Emperor had promised to Agassiz and his expedition came for them at Para. It was called the *Icamiaba* and was to be their home for many days. It was very different from the dirty little coastwise steamer that brought them from Rio to Para. It had good staterooms and even a big shallow bathtub made of copper into which yellow Amazon water would be poured. When days grew hot there was nothing like a cool bath — even in muddy water.

Everybody slept on deck. They had bought hammocks woven by the Amazonians out of plant fibers dyed in bright colors. Mrs. Agassiz's was brilliant pink. Over the hammocks went mosquito netting and through this they could look right up at the stars. There were new Southern constellations for those interested in astronomy to learn. By day an awning was drawn over the deck of the steamer and it became a sort of sitting room for everybody.

The mouth of the Amazon is two hundred and seven miles wide, so it is easy to understand why the Brazilians call it O *Rio Mar*, the River Sea. Agassiz said that there was so little current on the lower part of the Amazon that it was in fact much more like an inland sea than a

river. As the *Icamiaba* steamed along, they could see wooded shores. These were not actually shores, however, but countless small islands with waterways among them. The islands were solid green with here and there the top of a tall palm rising above the others, its fronds like feathers.

The steamer tied up at a small village every night. The engines burned wood and there was always the need to cut and load more wood because the pile on board burned fast. At every wharf there was a crowd of villagers, dark of skin with straight, jet-black hair. They were smiling and friendly and soon word spread upriver that foreigners were coming who would buy strange things. The people brought snakes, fishes, insects, flowers, birds and small animals which Agassiz was delighted to have. Mrs. Agassiz bought a parrot and several parakeets. The young students who had come with Agassiz could not resist the monkeys which were brought to the boat for sale. Soon each had a pet monkey of his own.

15

Amazon Adventure

RIVER BOATS STEAMED up the Amazon stopping at different villages each night. The *Icamiaba* had no regular schedule while Agassiz and his party were on board. When Agassiz heard of an inland lake he was free to visit it and the steamer would wait on the river for him. To go inland, Agassiz traveled in a local canoe. It had a straw-thatched cabin only about three feet high and six feet long. A second canoe carried supplies — a live sheep, a turkey and several hens. There were also barrels for collecting specimens and alcohol for preserving them. Burkhardt, the artist, went along as well as Ren Thayer and Mrs. Agassiz.

They set out at three in the morning, Brazilians paddling their canoes. Downriver they went for a short distance and then they turned into a narrow waterway. Great trees rose on each side, their roots rising from water and their tops arching overhead. The trees were hung from top to bottom with green vines and there was a heavy fragrance of flowers in the air. Sometimes there was a narrow strip of sky overhead and they watched it grow bright. The mournful cry of night-flying birds ceased and the birds that flew by day began to call with raucous, parrot-like voices. Now it was midmorning but in the forest the light was so dim that it always seemed like early evening. They paddled all day.

At night they reached the lake, with a village on the shore. Agassiz and his party were made welcome, for Major Coutinho, the Brazilian army officer, had arranged everything in advance. This jungle village was the first the Agassizs had seen and it pleased them very much. Houses had a frame of tree trunks lashed together with tough reeds from the lake. Most of them had no walls except woven mats which were hung up like curtains. These were made of palm leaves and the roofs were palm-leaf thatch. Each roof jutted out in front of the house to cover a sort of front porch where hammocks were hung and people gathered. There were no floors and the bare ground was neatly swept each morning.

During the hours around noon nobody did anything except lie in the hammocks in the shade of the palm-leaf thatch and talk or drop off to sleep. The faint breeze rustled in the dry palm leaves and made a pleasant sound. There were no doors to the houses and chickens, pigs and dogs wandered in and out.

The day's work began toward afternoon, and night was the time for fishing. Then, after work was done, it was time for a party. The people had a sort of guitar on which they played a kind of music with only a few notes. A big fire was built in the middle of an open space in front of the houses and here Agassiz and the other

Americans gathered. There was to be a dance, they were told. The music began. But the villagers were shy at first and Mrs. Agassiz had to persuade one of the girls to start the dancing.

The visitors from the United States had expected to see something like African dancing or like a North American Indian dance. But the dances they saw among the South American Indians were entirely different. Dancers stood opposite each other and moved only their feet in a slow, gliding motion. Once in a while they snapped their fingers in time with the music. Sometimes they glided in a circle, sometimes in squares. But they never moved very fast.

Now they asked Mrs. Agassiz if she would show them a dance of her own country. Mrs. Agassiz and Ren Thayer waltzed for them in the firelight because the waltz was everyone's favorite back home. But in a few minutes they found that they were feeling hot. Now they understood why the natives danced so slowly. Although there was usually a breeze in the evening, the Amazon country was much too damp and hot for North American dancing.

The inland lake proved full of fish. Burkhardt drew each newly discovered kind and painted it carefully in its natural colors. Fish preserved in alcohol turned an ugly brown and all the lovely colors would have been lost and forgotten but for Burkhardt's pictures. Agassiz examined and described the fish as fast as Burkhardt painted them. Ren Thayer collected flowers, beetles — everything he could lay hands on. Then back down the narrow waterways went Agassiz and his friends, to join the others on the steamship.

At Manaos, nine hundred miles from the Atlantic Ocean, the steamer *Icamiaba* had to turn back. Manaos is on the Rio Negro, or Black River, about twelve miles above the point where it joins the Amazon. From here, the Upper Amazon was too shallow for the *Icamiaba*. Agassiz longed to travel on and reach the source of the Amazon, high in the Andes in Peru. He would have loved the age of air travel when all three thousand three hundred miles of the Amazon could be covered in a short time. As it was, time was running out. Agassiz decided to take a smaller steamer which went down the Black River and then up the Solomoens, as the Upper Amazon was called.

The shores of the Upper Amazon were somewhat barren and muddy. Huge flocks of birds rose at the approach of the steamer, turtles poked their noses above water and now and then a plop and a splash told where a crocodile had slithered off a log. There were few settlements.

After six days, the little river steamer reached Tabatinga, the border town between Brazil and Peru. There was a fort with walls of dried mud where a few soldiers

were stationed. Here cargo would be transferred to a
Peruvian steamer and Agassiz and his party could go on
if they wanted to. Agassiz wanted particularly to get
closer to the Andes to see whether glaciers formed there,
as in Switzerland.

But there was a good reason for turning back. The
water in the Amazon was growing more shallow every
day. At flood time the water at Manaos rose sixty feet,
but when flood waters ran off, sand bars appeared, making navigation more and more difficult. Agassiz would
have to spend a whole year waiting for the next rainy
season unless he left while there was still water enough
to float the river boats.

There were still other reasons for turning back. At
Teffé, a town about three hundred miles below the border, Agassiz had found a small fish that had baby fish
in its mouth! Agassiz wanted to go back and study these
fish before the young ones all grew up and swam away.
It was the season too for turtle eggs and crocodile eggs
to hatch. He wanted to find some eggs and see them
hatch out if he could.

Agassiz soon saw how right he was when he decided
to go back. Everybody was packing up to leave the boat
at Teffé when there was a dull thump, the steamer jolted
and stopped short. They had struck a sand bar. The captain ordered full speed astern. The engines were re-
versed — but nothing happened. Teffé was supposed to

be only two hours away but steamers could be stranded for several weeks, Agassiz was told. Other passengers were worried because they might miss the last of the big boats which left Manaos for that season. But Agassiz was

anxious also because the fish-spawning season would be over.

About eight hours went by and it was five in the afternoon, with the steamer still aground. Then a sudden storm came up, with thunder and lightning and sheets of rain. The steamer swung as the wind hit her. The water rose suddenly — and they were free. Everyone began to cheer, but now it was discovered that an anchor which had been thrown out when they grounded was still stuck in the mud. The ship grounded again while the crew tried to raise the anchor and this time they were stuck all night. In the morning the ship was afloat again, but the rudder had been damaged and it took the crew all that day and the next night to rig up a new one. The steamer reached Teffé three days late but everyone was glad to get there at all!

Agassiz spent a month at Teffé, a town in many ways different from any other on the Amazon. Instead of thick forests or mud flats, there were green hills where cows and sheep were grazing. In front of the village was a broad sandy beach which would be covered with water during the rainy season. The houses, instead of being framed with logs and palm-thatched, were made of dried clay and roofed with tile. All had gardens with little picket fences around them.

A house was found that would hold Professor Agassiz and all his party. It was built one story high around a

patio where there were orange trees and a big tank for
turtles. Everybody in Teffé liked to eat turtles and almost every house had a tank for them. Agassiz promptly
filled the tank at his house with all sorts of live specimens. There was a large room where the men hung their
hammocks and a smaller room for Mrs. Agassiz. And
there was a closet where Agassiz kept two large live croc-
odiles. He rigged up a laboratory of course, with a big
table made of boards put across packing cases. His students made a swinging shelf to keep dried specimens,
such as beetles, out of the way of live ants which would
have eaten them.

Agassiz was not too late to find the fish that carried
its young in its mouth. He found that it had a sort of
sac for eggs and young fish. In the world of fish it was a
little like the opossum in the animal world. The *acara*,
the native people called this fish. Agassiz decided to name
it in honor of Emperor Dom Pedro II.

Some of Agassiz's young students had never been far
from home before. But he sent them out exploring alone
or by twos and threes in canoes with local people to
paddle for them. Agassiz was a teacher of more things
than ichthyology, the science of fish. He taught his boys
how to be self-reliant. First he would talk over the kind
of supplies needed. The boys already knew what specimens to look for and they studied what few maps there
were. Then the boys would set out before dawn

into country still marked "unexplored" on modern maps.

These boys came back from their expeditions looking like real explorers. William James wrote home that his mother would hardly recognize him. He wore only a cotton shirt and trousers, ragged from encounters with thorns. His hands were "all hacked up," he said. Once, at night, he said he heard a "tiger" roar not far from his tent and he was "some skeert," he admitted, making fun of himself. This beast was probably a jaguar.

The boys found they must wear shoes because a very unpleasant kind of insect bit their bare feet, making painful sores. Otherwise they returned from their expeditions well and strong.

Slowly the Agassiz party journeyed back down the Amazon. They stopped to collect roots of an enormous lily, one leaf of which was five feet across. Agassiz found the print of fossil ferns and he followed a low ridge of gravel and rounded stones which he knew had been left by a glacier. He urged Brazilian scientists to study the evidences of ice in Brazil.

Today scientists are still studying glacial evidences. They agree that there were comparatively small glaciers in prehistoric times in Brazil but they have not decided whether there was a great sheet of ice, as in North America.

There is always something new to study in natural history. Agassiz sent more than eighty thousand specimens from Brazil to his Museum of Comparative Zoology in Cambridge. But today roads are being bulldozed through the jungle. Air travel has cut down the immense Brazilian distances and much that is new, especially in the field of minerals, is being discovered.

16

The Voyage of the Hassler

So MANY SPECIMENS ARRIVED in Cambridge and so
many students wanted to study at the Lawrence Scientific School that Agassiz knew he must have an addition
built for his museum. It would cost a good deal and most
people would have had trouble raising enough money.
But Agassiz thought that there was nothing more important than natural science. He told the Massachusetts
legislature that the young scientists he was training could
help farmers by showing them how to fight insects that
attacked their crops. Geologists studying natural science
would be able to tell where oil or copper might be found.
Everyone was eager to hear Agassiz lecture on Brazil and
they looked forward to the day when they might go to
a new wing of the museum to see some of the things he
had brought home. The legislature voted money and people contributed to a drive to raise funds. Soon another
section of the Museum of Comparative Zoology was
built on Oxford Street.

People said it was easy for Agassiz to raise money. As
a matter of fact, he worked very hard at it. His lectures
were never read from a manuscript but told to the audience without notes. This meant that they had to be very
carefully thought out beforehand and remembered.

Agassiz gave dinner parties and went to parties where people wanted to hear about Brazil. He liked people and he had a wonderful time. But he got tired and his doctor told him he ought to take a rest.

Agassiz's idea of a rest was to go out looking for more specimens for his collections. He had heard that there were fossil sea creatures right in the middle of the United States where now there is certainly no ocean. Agassiz knew why the fossils were there. More than three million years ago, the United States was a watery place. Volcanic mountains had risen along the Atlantic coast but the sea flowed in through the Gulf of Mexico and flooded the Mississippi Valley, the Great Lakes area and more besides. When Agassiz heard that fossils had been found by workmen on the new Union Pacific railroad, he wanted nothing so much as to go to see them for himself.

A friend of Agassiz's was a Congressman from Massachusetts. It was not long before this member of Congress decided he ought to check up on the progress of the railroad — and take Agassiz along. The year was 1868 and the Union Pacific was built only as far as Green River Station in Wyoming. However, the road was much more than halfway across the continent and had reached the southern spurs of the Rocky Mountains.

General William T. Sherman, now commanding general of the United States Army, joined Agassiz's party with an escort of cavalry as they crossed part of Kansas and Nebraska. There were ambulances which had been used in the Civil War for the Congressman and Agassiz to ride in because, although rails had been laid, there were as yet no trains. Indian war parties might possibly be met with, so that a cavalry escort was needed.

Agassiz felt his strength returning as he traveled across the country. Ever since he first came to the United States he had wanted to see the West. He could laugh at himself now, for imagining that such a journey would take just a few days. Arriving at last at Green River Station, Agassiz saw limestone deposits full of fish and insect imprints. Workmen on the railroad brought him specimens and promised to look for more. And Agassiz had the joy of finding trilobites himself. These sea creatures were much older than the reptiles, older even than fish, and quite beautiful to look at. Trilobites were ancient relatives of the lobsters of today.

An old trapper told of still more strange discoveries. Farther on and higher in the mountains there were "grizzly bears turned to stone," the old man said. There were "bones heavy as rocks." Thinking that people didn't believe him, he brought in a bag full of fossil bones and among them was a well-preserved skull. It really looked very much like the skull of a bear. But the creature had been a prehistoric reptile. These creatures belonged to a later period in prehistory and Agassiz

longed to go with the old trapper and see where he got the fossil bones. But the place was sixty miles away. Agassiz would have to go there on horseback and there was no time for such a long trip. Reluctantly Agassiz turned back, leaving the discovery of huge fossil reptiles to other scientists but bringing home his trilobites.

Agassiz did not go straight home to Cambridge. He stopped off in Ithaca, New York, where Cornell University was just getting started. Agassiz had a great deal to do with making Cornell outstanding in natural science. He made a speech at the opening ceremonies telling the students what a wonderful opportunity they were going to have to study astronomy, botany, geology — all the subjects which other colleges were inclined to neglect.

There was time for a walk before Agassiz took a train for home. And as he never crossed a brook without looking to see what happened to be living in the water, he was soon down on his knees on a rock. A boy crossing the bridge over the brook stopped to stare at the grown man, all dressed in city clothes. Was he playing in the brook? The man looked up and smiled. "Come and let me show you something," Agassiz said.

The boy went down into the brook-bed with Agassiz and soon he learned that the fish he saw were "sticklebacks." You could keep them in a glass bowl if you wanted to. Agassiz said they would eat snails. The boy learned where turtles go in winter and where to look for frogs' eggs in spring. Perhaps he was late to school that afternoon. Or maybe he had been sent on an errand which took a long time. Perhaps someday he would go to Cornell and be a scientist.

There were two things that Agassiz had especially in mind these days. One was to persuade young people to be scientists. Another was to start museums in towns and cities all over the United States. Then Americans would not go around their country forgetting to look at birds, ignorantly destroying wildflowers and never learning about rocks, or stars, or depths of ocean. If he could get museums started everywhere, all sorts of good things might happen. People might be taught to stop wasting natural resources. There would be opportunities for people to start a hobby of collecting specimens. And there would be jobs as museum directors for Agassiz's best students.

The Smithsonian Institution at Washington, D. C., was established at about the time when Agassiz first came to the United States. He became a member of the governing board and was able to carry out some of his best ideas. One of these was to have natural scientists sent out with the government surveyors who were exploring and establishing the boundaries of the United States. Some of Agassiz's students went on these exploring trips. They made a big contribution to the knowledge of this country — and of course they brought back specimens for Agassiz's museum as well as for the Smithsonian.

In 1871, Agassiz himself was invited to go on a government expedition. The steamer *Hassler* was especially built for deep-sea dredging so that new charts of coastal waters could be made. Mrs. Agassiz was invited to go with her husband and she kept a record of the journey just as she had done in Brazil. All the fish and deep-sea creatures brought up in the dredges would be shared by the Smithsonian and Agassiz's own museum.

The *Hassler* was to sail through the Strait of Magellan from the Atlantic Ocean to the Pacific. Not even Magellan himself could have felt any more eager for such a voyage than Louis Agassiz.

The *Hassler* was supposed to set out in August but there were delays on the part of the shipbuilders. She finally left Boston December 4 in the midst of the first snowstorm of the winter. Her first port of call was St. Thomas in the West Indies, where the cruise ships now go. Some of the modern cruise ships are over 32,000 tons. The *Hassler* was 360 tons. They called her a steamer, but she was rigged as a three-masted schooner and her steam engines were just to help her along. She pitched heavily in the Atlantic swells but Agassiz did not mind. He was a good sailor and he said he liked the ship because it was so small that he could almost catch fish over the side with his hands.

As before, on the way to Brazil, Agassiz was interested in the temperature of the water. When the thermometer showed that they had reached the warm waters of the Gulf Stream, he turned most of his attention to the gulfweed (sargassum) which floats on the current.

A sailor brought Agassiz a ball of sargassum "about the size of two fists." The ball of seaweed proved to be fastened together by fine thread-like material. When he put the ball into a glass bowl and looked at it with a magnifying glass, Agassiz could see that the threads were beaded at intervals. The beads were fish eggs. They were about the size of a pinhead, but Agassiz's pocket lens enlarged them so that he could see "two eyes and a tail bent over the back of the body." The fish hatched out next day.

But tiny fish all look very much alike and Agassiz could not tell what kind these would be that came from the seaweed nest. Then he remembered studying color cells in newly hatched fish. The *Hassler* had a microscope on board, strong enough so that Agassiz could examine these fish for color cells and prove that the fish would grow up to be a kind of tarpon — a game fish popular with deep-sea fishermen.

The first success, the discovery of the fishes' nest, was the last for some time. The machinery for dredging on board the *Hassler* was not strong enough to bring up sea creatures from the deep water off St. Thomas. Cables broke, engines quit and nets were lost. But some day Agassiz's son Alexander would equip a ship of his own and dredge these waters. Meanwhile Agassiz tried to content himself by collecting sponges. Natural sponges were once commonly sold in drugstores and most people never realized that so-called "bath sponges" were really sea animals. In tropical waters they grew in all sorts of shapes and colors and of course Agassiz was fascinated by them.

The *Hassler* sailed from the West Indies to Rio de Janeiro and then on down the east coast of South America. San Matias Gulf bites into the coast of Argentina for a hundred miles or more. Near here, Agassiz found rocks that were solid masses of fossils. He collected "superb specimens," he said. There were "immense fossil oyster shells and perfectly preserved sea urchins all crowded together in big boulders" and it seemed a shame the *Hassler* would hold only a few chunks chipped off these rocks.

The dredgings, the soundings and the excursions ashore along the coast of South America were all exciting. But everyone was looking forward to the Strait of Magellan. Nearly four months after leaving Boston, the *Hassler* rounded Cape Virgenes and steamed into the Strait. It was March, but the weather was like a crisp October day in New England. Skies were blue and the tide was at the flood.

17

Glaciers and Iguanas

THE STRAIT OF MAGELLAN is about three hundred and fifty miles long and at its widest point it is only seventy miles across. Winds roar through it and the channel is dangerous with deep water giving way to shoal without warning. The only permanent settlement was called Sandy Point, where there was a coal mine.

A railroad wound its way up steep wooded hills to the mine but there were no engines. Horses pulled the small railroad cars. Into one of the cars climbed Agassiz, delighted with the chance to take another dangerous ride. The cliffs where men had cut into the rock were full of fossils, just as he had hoped they might be. "Look," he cried, "an oyster bank right there above the track!" At first the mine superintendent thought the scientist had lost his mind. Then he saw that, sure enough, there were oysters which seemed to have turned to stone. Workmen got off the train and chipped specimens for Agassiz as he explained to them how fossils were made. As usual, everyone promised to help him hunt for specimens.

The *Hassler* sailed on, traveling by day and finding anchorage in some lonely bay when night came. The channel was so hard to follow that it was dangerous to sail at night but the bays were uncharted too. The captain had only a general idea of where he would find safe shelter. While the chart-makers aboard ship were busy, Agassiz went ashore. He hoped to meet some "aborigines."

At first it seemed as if there were no native people on the bleak shores of the Strait. Then Agassiz found curious semicircular houses made out of saplings stripped of their branches. The ends of these sticks were set in the ground, their tops pulled inward and tied together. Other flexible twigs were woven in and out among them. Each of these huts looked like half of a wicker basket turned bottom upwards. In front of the little huts were piles of empty mussel shells and the ashes of fires. To Agassiz's disappointment, the Indians had gone away.

A few days later, however, the *Hassler* was anchored in another cove. Agassiz, with two or three assistants, went ashore, pitched a tent and built a fire. They collected ferns and lichens along a little brook. They found starfish and sea urchins in a tidal pool. It was afternoon when they sat down in front of their fire to rest. And then around the point came a boat full of people. There were men, women and children but only the men, six or seven of them, came ashore. They were short with thin arms and legs and they wore the skins of animals. But the skins were not made into clothing. They were just hung on a thong around the neck or from a thong around the waist. Some of the men were naked to the

waist although it was so cold that Agassiz and his party
were bundled up in winter clothes.

The Indians came up to the fire and spread out their
hands to it. *"Tabac, tabac!"* they shouted — "Tobacco,
tobacco" — all of them yelling at once as though they
thought the strangers on their shore were deaf. Agassiz
welcomed them joyfully but for once his friendly smile
was not returned. Sharp black eyes peered through
coarse, straight black hair. Mouths were grim and the
men leered in a way that would have frightened most
people. Agassiz got out the remains of a picnic lunch
and handed around pork and ship's biscuit. The men
snatched at the food and ate like hungry animals. Agassiz found some tobacco which he gave them.

Now the Indian leader sat down on a stone and began
to sing. His song had only two or three notes to it but
plenty of rhythm, and the others kept time by clapping
their hands and thumping their feet on the ground.
Judging by the expression of their faces and by their
gestures the song was about the visitors who had come in
the ship. The song ended suddenly. There was silence
and the singer looked disappointed, so Agassiz and his
friends began to applaud. This pleased the Indians and
now they laughed and clapped too.

The ship's gun went off, signaling the shore party to
return. Folding their tent and gathering up their equipment and specimens, Agassiz and his friends went down

the beach to the boat which was sent out from the *Hassler* for them. Their new friends followed closely, shouting "*Tabac, tabac!*" The Indians got into their own boat and paddled over to the ship, their women and children joining in the shout of "*Tabac!*"

The Indians would have liked to come aboard the *Hassler* but they were made to keep their distance. Some tobacco, ship's biscuits, bright calico and glass beads were lowered down to them. They fought over their presents and snatched at them. "They're like wild animals," Agassiz said. But the Indians gave bows, arrows and baskets in return for the presents. They kept on shouting "*Tabac*" until the steamer began to leave their boat behind. Then they sang their strange monotonous song again.

The *Hassler* continued along the Strait of Magellan, her captain passing a bay where he might have anchored for the night. But the breeze was strong and he thought he could go farther before nightfall. And then, without warning, the breeze became a gale. One of those sudden windstorms for which the Strait was famous had struck the *Hassler*. The channel was instantly a welter of white foam. A sail split with a terrible rending sound and the shouts of the captain, ordering his crew, could hardly be heard above the roar of the wind. Even with the help of the engines, the *Hassler* could not be held on course and the captain decided to come about.

The *Hassler* swung and as she came broadside to the wind it seemed as if she would certainly capsize. But somehow she made the turn and now the wind was at her heels and she flew along with terrifying speed. They reached Borja Bay in record time and by a combination of good luck and good seamanship the *Hassler* entered the harbor. Inside, there was calm water! On board the *Hassler,* they could still hear the wind roaring in the Strait but rocky headlands safely sheltered them.

A great glacier came down into a bay in the Strait of Magellan. Almost all the explorers of the Strait mentioned this glacier, having seen it from a distance. But no one had ever visited it and it had no name. Agassiz longed to be the first to reach the glacier and about nine o'clock one morning the *Hassler* put in at Glacier Bay. A boat was lowered and Professor and Mrs. Agassiz and four scientists rowed ashore. Glacier Bay was too deep for anchorage and the *Hassler* went on to nearby Playa Parda Cove.

There was a rough, pebbly beach, then a strip of forest with the glacier rising white and glistening beyond it. From the deck of the ship, the forest looked gray as though all the trees were dead. But Agassiz saw that the dead trees were only on the edge of the forest close to the beach. Beyond were trees as green as those on the Amazon. Every trunk, every branch and every fallen log was covered with bright green moss. There were pink trum-

pet-shaped flowers hanging from a vine. And there were
red bell-shaped flowers growing close to the ground. The
forest at the southern tip of South America looked like
a woodland at home in springtime.

It was not far through the woods to the glacier but
the walking was rough. Agassiz thought the journey
would be too hard for his wife so he went on ahead. At
almost every step, he sank almost to his knees in damp
moss with wet rotting logs below it. Smooth rocks were
moss-covered, making the footing treacherous as they
followed an icy river which ran out of the glacier. Sometimes one bank was so steep that they had to cross to the
other side, cutting trees and throwing them over the
river for a bridge. Sometimes they had to hack a path-
way through the trees. It took over an hour to walk less
than a mile but at last they could see the gleam of ice
ahead.

Suddenly they came out into the open and there was
a wall of pure white ice. The glacier was at least a mile
and a half wide and at the center, where they stood, there
were deep caves of blue, transparent ice.

There were famous glacial caves in Switzerland which
Agassiz had seen but he had never before seen larger or
more beautiful caves than these. Swiss glaciers are often
filled with sand and gravel at their lower end where they
have begun to melt. This one was clean and white, its
surface like glass.

Agassiz and his fellow scientists began to measure height and thickness of ice, making notes of all they saw. The route through the woods had been so rough that Agassiz was sure his wife could not make the trip although he had sent someone back to help her. He was disappointed because he wanted her to share his pleasure in this beautiful river of ice. And then he heard a halloo. There at the edge of the woods was Mrs. Agassiz. She had made it after all and she said afterwards that she never forgot the look of joyful surprise on Agassiz's face. The American girl he had married always proved to be his good companion. She loved all the things he cared most about and she had the courage to go with him in all his adventuring.

Agassiz and his wife climbed the glacier as far as they could, cutting steps in the ice as they went along. "We looked at the ice till we were tired," said Mrs. Agassiz. Then one of the young students built a good campfire among the stones and gravel of the moraine. They sat down to warm themselves and dry their clothes. They had reached a glacier which no one else had ever so much as approached before and it proved to be the most beautiful even Agassiz had ever seen. Now they suddenly realized that they were hungry.

Once more there came a shout from the strip of forest. This time it was the captain of the *Hassler* with some of his crew and they were carrying a hamper of food. They had brought ham and sardines, potato salad and ship's biscuit.

Back to the *Hassler* went the tired explorers that night. They enjoyed a good dinner aboard ship and they gave the glacier a name, by right of being the first to visit it. In honor of their ship, they named it the "Hassler Glacier," and so it appears on modern maps.

Agassiz and his fellow scientists spent several days studying the Hassler Glacier. Then the *Hassler* sailed on and finally emerged on the Pacific Ocean and turned north along the far west coast of South America. They had spent more than a month in the Strait, a region of snow-capped mountains, deep bays and turbulent channel sailing. The ship needed repairs and so, on the 15th of April she put in at Concepción Bay in Chile. Agassiz decided to travel by road along the coast of Chile. At Valparaiso the *Hassler* awaited him and he went back on board. Now he was off for the Galápagos Islands, and the *Hassler* arrived there on the 10th of June.

The Galápagos Islands are in the Pacific Ocean about six hundred miles off the coast of Ecuador and they lie right on the equator. They are volcanic and perhaps they are the tops of once high mountains in a land that has sunk below the sea. The Galápagos are exciting to naturalists because animals now alive there look like the animals that were alive when dinosaurs roamed the earth.

The *Hassler* touched first at Clark Island but not even

Agassiz could explore very far inland. Giant cactus plants with huge thorns grew everywhere. A path among them had to be cut with an ax. The heat was intense. But on the beach were land crabs, the largest Agassiz had ever seen. They were bright red.

On sailed the *Hassler* to Albemarle Island. The crater of a volcano rose about four thousand feet in the center of Albemarle and there were about fifty other smaller, chimney-like holes in the rocks where once fire and melted red-hot rock had roared out. These craters were cold now and the lava had hardened into rock in curious shapes. Surf, dashing on blocks of lava, at first kept the *Hassler* from entering the bay. While waiting for the sea to grow calm, Agassiz watched the water, over the rail of the ship. Iguanas, some of them five feet long, were swimming around. These marine lizards were jet black with queer-looking knobs on their heads. Along their backs they had black spines. They looked ugly and dangerous but when Agassiz caught some of them they proved to be gentle and easy to tame. They never had any idea of biting anyone.

Next day the scientists went ashore from Iguana Cove. They found holes in the ground in all directions where the land iguanas had their burrows. The land iguanas were only about two feet long and were colored red and orange, Agassiz said. The sailors from the ship ran after these lizards and caught as many of them as they could, hoping to make pets of them. But these lizards could bite!

There was a superstition that iguanas could be tamed if someone would sing to them. Mrs. Agassiz saw a lizard running around a tree and she came slowly up to it, singing softly. The lizard stopped running quite so fast. Then it ran slower and slower until it finally stopped. Mrs. Agassiz was sure she had tamed it — until she came close. Then she saw that one of the sailors had already caught it and had tied a rope around its neck and fastened the rope to the tree. The lizard had wound the rope around the tree until it could run no farther. Everyone laughed at Mrs. Agassiz and she felt rather silly. But she was a good sport and joined in the laughter.

At James Island, they saw flamingos, their red wings tipped with black. It seemed a shame to kill anything so beautiful but roast flamingo proved very good to eat.

The Galápagos Islands are famous for their giant tortoises. Agassiz discovered that each island had a different kind living on it and some of the tortoises weighed up to five hundred pounds. These too were good to eat and the crews from whaling ships, hungry for fresh food, had killed many of them. But Agassiz brought home handsome specimens for the Smithsonian Institution and his own Museum of Comparative Zoology.

Later, a good many giant Galápagos tortoises were brought alive to this country. They live to be over a hun-

dred years old and can be found in most large collections
of living reptiles. The New York Zoological Park has
several, which are gentle and intelligent. When they
want to get out of their inside rooms they hammer on

the doors with the front of their heavy shell until an attendant comes to let them out so they can bask in the sun. They have a saddle-shaped shell and one old fellow would let children ride on his back. An apple fastened to a stick and held in front of him would make him move slowly along.

Agassiz would have loved to bring live tortoises and iguanas home with him but the problem of transportation was too difficult. He sent home over two hundred and fifty barrels and cases of preserved specimens. There were thirty thousand fish and uncounted numbers of insects, worms, sea urchins and starfish. In all, probably more than a hundred thousand items were collected.

Charles Darwin had visited the Galápagos Islands during his voyage around the world — a voyage lasting from December, 1831, until October, 1836. It was Darwin who observed that the animals living on the islands were like prehistoric animals of Europe. This discovery formed part of the proof of the theory of evolution and of course Agassiz had read all that Darwin had written. It is hard for one scientist to admit that he is wrong and another is right, and so Agassiz really hoped to find that Darwin had made serious mistakes. But a study of the Galápagos specimens showed that Darwin had been right all along. Now Agassiz set to work to write an article to give credit to his former rival and to agree with Darwin in all but a few details.

18

Museum Man

As soon as Agassiz got back home to Cambridge, he started a new project. Natural history was just beginning to be taught in the schools. Before Louis Agassiz came to the United States there was hardly ever a lesson about birds and how to tell what kind of bird might be singing outside the schoolroom window. There were no glass bowls with tadpoles in them for grade-school children to watch. A boy or girl who brought an interesting rock to school had no chance to look it up in a nature book and learn about it. But Louis Agassiz had been in the United States for twenty-six years now. He had taught people everywhere to enjoy the world out of doors and to study it. More than anyone else, he was the man who gave nature-study classes a start — but few people knew how to teach this new subject.

For a long time, Agassiz had been thinking about a summer school for teachers and for anyone else interested in natural science. When he got home to Massachusetts he told the state legislature about his idea. A reporter put Agassiz's speech in a newspaper and a man in New York named John Anderson read about it. Mr. Anderson wrote to Agassiz. Within a week after he had made his speech, Agassiz had an island called Penikese in

Buzzards Bay with buildings on it which Mr. Anderson
had given him for the school. Mr. Anderson also gave
money for a new building, for furniture and scientific instruments so that teachers could study natural
science.

Agassiz was always optimistic. The island was given
to him in March and he was sure that he could open the
Anderson School of Natural History by the 8th of July.
He wrote a letter telling about his plans and had copies
of it sent out to teachers all over the country.

On the 4th of July, the Agassizs set out for New Bedford, Massachusetts. A boat was to take them from there
to Penikese Island the next day. But at the hotel in New
Bedford they found the architect of the new building
waiting for them. This building, where students at the
new school were to sleep, had walls and a roof but that
was all, said the architect.

"In four days, fifty-eight people will arrive at the
island," Agassiz told him. "They must have a place to
sleep."

"Impossible!" the architect said. A barn was being
built over into a dining hall and that wasn't ready either.
The people would have no place to eat or sleep. But
Agassiz said he wasn't worried!

A Cornell professor had been invited to come to Penikese to help with the teaching and he had brought his
family along. They arrived at the New Bedford hotel

and so did a teacher who had made a mistake about the date when the school was to open. Agassiz asked them all if they would like to go out to the island and help get the school ready. They said they would.

Next day, in a dismal rain, they set out for Penikese. On the dock at the island they found one of Mrs. Agassiz's nephews. "You look like a shipwrecked sailor," she told him, laughing. He said he had managed to get the new beds and the rest of the new furniture in out of the rain. But he had gotten soaked and he was covered with mud.

Agassiz was still sure that everything would be ready, but before the boat left for the mainland carpenters crowded on board. It was Saturday afternoon and they were leaving. Some said they would be back but others said they were really fishermen. They had taken the carpentry job just to fill in and they were going back to their trawlers.

The rain was still coming down. Agassiz and his friends went up to the old house where Mr. Anderson used to live and cooked themselves some ham and eggs, and now everybody began to share some of Agassiz's optimism. Other workmen had planned to leave next day, but when they found out who Agassiz was and what he was planning to do on the island, they agreed to stay and work.

On Sunday Mrs. Agassiz, the Cornell professor's wife and the teacher washed all the dishes and glassware for the school. The carpenters got floors and a staircase finished in the new building. The old barn was cleaned and they began to lay a new floor in it.

The barn was to be used as a lecture room as well as a dining hall. When the day came for the school to open, the floor was not quite finished. Agassiz had chairs moved in anyway, for the students and the guests whom he had invited to the opening ceremonies. He heard the boat whistle down at the dock and looked around. The carpenters were just driving the last nail!

Agassiz had invited the Governor of Massachusetts and members of the legislature to the opening of the Anderson School of Natural History. He had invited prominent businessmen, people interested in education, writers and newspapermen. Wildflowers that grew on the island decorated the room. Even the weather helped out, for the sun was shining and the water around the island of Penikese was a deep, calm blue.

There was no prepared program. Agassiz trusted to the ideas that would come to him. He stood up and looked at the people — those who had come to give the school a good send-off and those who had come to study. Beyond them was the sea which Agassiz had loved even before he saw it. "Let us join in silently asking God's blessing upon our work together," he said. No one who was there ever forgot that moment, and later John Greenleaf Whittier wrote a poem about it.

Agassiz's summer at Penikese was one of the happiest in a happy life. These students had come to him because they wanted to be able to teach children about the wonderful outdoor world, and this pleased him. He took the teachers roaming around the rocks on the island in the morning and taught them to use their eyes. They brought in specimens and in the afternoon he taught them to use microscopes in the classroom in the old barn. In the evening he lectured. No one thought this was a long day or that there was too much work to do. It was so interesting and such fun.

The summer on the island was over all too soon. Agassiz went back to his college classes at Harvard, and this kind of teaching he liked too. He was happy as long as he could show his specimens to his students and talk to them and teach them to think for themselves. But he did not like to sit at a desk and write, and some of the books he started were never finished.

Agassiz had dreamed of one huge museum where specimens of everything living or prehistoric could be studied. He had been, after all, a boy from Switzerland, a small country where people walked from one village to another. But now he was a citizen of the United States and his ideas had changed. He knew and loved a big

country and now he realized that there should be many
fine American museums in many towns and cities. Once
he had wanted all the best specimens for the Museum of
Comparative Zoology in Cambridge. But now he wanted
other museums to share the treasures found in different
parts of the country.

When Agassiz first saw the famous dinosaur tracks in
the shale along the bank of the Connecticut River near
Holyoke, Massachusetts, he wanted to buy all the rocks
with prehistoric tracks in them for his museum at Harvard. Then he went to Amherst College to call on a fellow natural scientist and saw what a fine collection of
prehistoric tracks were already assembled at Amherst.
"You are far ahead of me here," Agassiz said. "I shall not
attempt to make a better collection."

A great dead whale was washed up on the shore of
Long Island. Its skeleton would make a fine addition to
the Museum of Comparative Zoology, Agassiz thought.
Then he found that the Museum of Natural History in
New York wanted the whale. He wrote at once saying
they could have it.

All of Agassiz's first students had now left school. A
great many of them were already famous. There was
Frederic Ward Putnam — "Putty," his friends called
him. He left Agassiz's classroom to become curator of
Vertebrata (animals with a backbone) at the Essex In-
stitute in his home town of Salem, Massachusetts. Even-

tually he came back to work at the great museum which
Agassiz founded.

Addison Emery Verrill became Professor of Zoology
at Yale University as soon as he finished his courses with
Agassiz. Nathaniel Southgate Shaler, the student who
stared so long and hard at the little fish in Agassiz's laboratory, became Professor of Geology at Harvard and
Dean of the Lawrence Scientific School. Edward Syl-
vester Morse taught at the University of Tokyo.

Agassiz's son Alexander, after receiving a degree at
Harvard, a degree in mining engineering and another in
zoology at the Lawrence Scientific School, went into
mining on the Great Lakes. Soon he had money enough
so that he could afford to be a natural scientist and pay
for all his own expeditions. This was what he had always

wanted to do. He took his father's place at the museum while his father went to Brazil and the Strait of Magellan. Eventually, he headed the museum.

Ida, Agassiz's eldest daughter, married Major Henry Lee Higginson, a Civil War hero. They both loved music and worked together to establish the Boston Symphony orchestra. Pauline married Quincy Adams Shaw of Boston. Like her father, Pauline loved to teach, and she organized kindergartens for blind children. Both girls were always interested in their father's museum and helped to raise money to build still more, still larger buildings for his collections.

Louis Agassiz worked hard and played hard. He never seemed to take any rest. After his busy summer on Penikese Island, his doctor reminded him that he was at about the age when most people retire. But Agassiz's idea of retirement would have been to travel to some half-civilized part of the world and search for specimens of fish or fossils. His expeditions to the Amazon and the Strait of Magellan and his mountain climbing in the Alps had all been "vacations."

In December, 1873, there was a big party at Agassiz's house. His children were there and his grandchildren. He loved to play with little children. He would ride them around on his back and call them special pet names such as "Echinoderm" — little "Sea urchin." A famous man is usually called by his last name alone and so it was with

Agassiz. His grandchildren tried to call him "Agassiz" like everyone else. But "Gashy" was as close as they could get to it when they were little.

The day after the party Agassiz felt tired and came home early from the laboratory in the great museum which he had built. He thought he would lie down awhile on the couch in his study. He would soon feel rested, and meanwhile he had fine things to think about. There was the museum — a boy's dream come true. There were still many places he had yet to explore. In the world of natural science there would always be something to see and something to learn. Louis Agassiz fell asleep and never woke. He died December 14, 1873.

A glacial stone from the valley of the Aar was brought from Switzerland to be Agassiz's monument. They put his name in bronze on the house where he was born. But natural history museums all over the United States are his real monument. He would love to see the museums of today with their towering prehistoric animals, their wonderfully real scenes showing animals, trees and flowers, even birds, snakes and beetles from distant lands. New discoveries about outer space and the ocean depths would delight him. But Agassiz would like best of all to see the young people who come to museums to learn about the history of their world — and then go out to use their own eyes.

By means of his studies of fish and of glaciers, Agassiz

proved that there was an ice age and that the earth is very old. "I have taught my students to observe," he said. There will always be something new to learn and Louis Agassiz opened many doors leading out into the exciting modern world of natural science.

INDEX